Longing to PRAY

Longing to PRAY

How the Psalms Teach Us
to Talk with God

J. ELLSWORTH KALAS

Abingdon Press
Nashville

LONGING TO PRAY
HOW THE PSALMS TEACH US TO TALK WITH GOD

Copyright © 2006 by Abingdon Press

Library of Congress Cataloging-in-Publication Data

Kalas, J. Ellsworth, 1923–
Longing to pray : how the Psalms teach us to talk with God / J. Ellsworth Kalas.
    p. cm.
ISBN 0-687-49512-1 (binding: adhesive : alk. paper)
    1. Bible. O.T. Psalms—Criticism, interpretation, etc. 2. Friendship—Biblical teaching. 3. Prayer—Biblical teaching. I. Title.

BS1430.6.F73K35 2006
242'.5—dc22

                                                              2005029636

06 07 08 09 10 11 12 13 14 15—10 9 8 7 6 5 4 3 2 1

MANUFACTURED IN THE UNITED STATES OF AMERICA

Contents

Foreword

I thought it was a discontinuity in logic when I heard several years ago that in a certain European country more people prayed than believed in God. But when I thought a bit longer, I wasn't surprised. Prayer is so instinctive to our human nature that no laws of logic are involved. The doubter or the unbeliever feels that if there isn't a God, there ought to be; there ought, that is, to be Someone somewhere who cares about us enough to listen to our needs, and who might even be pleased to communicate with us. We may not pray often, and we may not pray well, but all of us want, somehow, some way, to pray.

And most of us wish we could pray well. The disciples of Jesus said, "Teach us to pray"; we echo, "Me, too." Some of us go on prayer retreats or attend special sessions where an "expert" teaches us about prayer. If we're fortunate enough to know someone who seems demonstrably close to God, we may even dare to ask his or her secret.

This little book invites us to study with some ancient experts in prayer, the persons who wrote the book of Psalms. We haven't read long in the psalms before we realize that the authors were altogether human, with a massive catalog of troubles, inconsistencies, and questions. Their lives were marked by breathtaking highs and lows, with sometimes only a few paragraphs between. But with all of that, they were saints. They left us with the greatest collection of prayers in the possession of our human race.

What was their secret? I believe it was the quality of their friendship with God. And of course the language of that friendship is prayer. The psalmists don't give us any formula for effective praying. They don't offer a set of rules. But if we read their prayers carefully, we will learn something of their secret, the secret of the Ultimate Friendship. I hope this book will help us along on that very special journey.

—*J. Ellsworth Kalas*

Chapter One

The Ultimate Friendship

I have lived long enough to know that very few things in this world, if any, matter as much as friendship. Friendships, like dogs, come in so many shapes and sizes that one can hardly believe that the same generic name applies to all. *Friendship* can mean everything from the person we know only at the checkout counter or at the dry-cleaning shop (in many cases we hardly know their names) to persons who are so much a part of our lives that it's hard to imagine life without them. Each year I realize with more intensity the truth of John Donne's words that "any man's death diminishes me"; that even casual friendships make up more of the fabric of our lives than we realize, and that our great friendships are simply invaluable.

Thousands of times I have remembered the words of Grace Bagby, a high-school English teacher, and hundreds of times I have quoted her: If you get one true friend in this lifetime, she told our class, just one true friend, you're rich. I have been rich several times by Miss Bagby's definition, and I am rich in that fashion today. I thank God nearly every day for such friendships, and I cherish such wealth for you.

But I've also lived long enough to know that one shouldn't expect too much from any human friend. That's because our human friends *are* human. They get tired—tired in general, and sometimes tired of us. They have problems of their own. They are limited in strength, patience, and understanding. One shouldn't expect too much of any human friend.

You and I need another Friendship. We need God. When Blaise Pascal said that there is in every human heart a God-shaped void that only God can fill, he was describing the friendship that matters most; indeed, that matters eternally. And for this friendship with God, the language of communication is *prayer*. This language is so instinctive to us that we humans pray whether we are religious or not. Some don't pray much, and as a result, they don't have much of a friendship, but I suspect that everyone sends out a prayer now and then. Some years ago a public opinion survey in a major European country revealed that in that country more people prayed than believed in God, which is to say that people yearn for this friendship even when they resent, question, or deny the Friend.

As for me, I confess without apology that this is the friendship without which I could not survive. I have read of the saints who have passed through the "dark night of the soul," periods of time when they could not in any way sense the reality or the presence of God. Call me a spiritual coward, but I do not wish to reach such a level of saintliness that God would entrust me to pass through such an experience of holy absence. My need for the Divine Friendship is too great. I cherish open communication with God. Above everything, I need this friendship.

The biblical book of Psalms is the book of this eternal friendship. It provides more understanding for this friendship than any other single book in the Bible. More than that (and here is the point and reason for this book), it gives us the *language* of the friendship, and it does so in simple and wonderful ways. For this reason, I see the book of Psalms as the best place to learn how to pray.

What do I mean by this? If you have read the book of Psalms, you know that it never gives instruction in prayer. In no place does it tell us how to approach God; in no place, indeed, does it offer a defined pattern such as we have in what we call "the Lord's Prayer." So how is it that I consider the psalms to be the premier place of instruction in prayer?

I can best explain what I mean by describing a scene that was a commonplace until cookbooks became a standard best-seller in American bookstores. At a time when recipes were more often kept on slips of paper or pasted in dough-spattered books, or in some cases simply stored in memory, girls just into their teens approached a grandmother (or perhaps a great aunt) with a conversation that ran like this.

"Granny, would you give me the recipe for your baking-powder biscuits?"

"Oh, *pshaw*, there's nothing to it. First, you get yourself a bowl."

"How big a bowl?"

"Oh, you'll know. Just the right size for what you're going to do. Then you pour in some flour."

"How much?"

"Well, you can tell by how it fills the bottom of the bowl. Then stir in some milk."

"How much, Granny?"

"Just enough so that when you stir it, it feels right."

"I'll tell you what, Granny, how would it be if I just went to the kitchen with you, and followed you around and wrote down what you're doing while you make a batch of biscuits?"

Quite simply, that's what I want to do in this book. I want us to go to the kitchen with the great, very human souls who gave us the book of Psalms, and watch them as they pray. As we watch them, we will learn how they prayed, and we will discover that their way of praying is not limited to a certain time or culture. Their prayers provide us with the language of the eternal Friendship.

But first, let me tell you a little about this book of Psalms.

With 150 chapters, this is the longest book in the Bible. By position, it falls almost exactly in the middle of the Bible—that is, the middle of the combined Old and New Testaments. I am not suggesting that this position is divinely ordained, but it is wonderfully appropriate, because if there is any single book that is at the heart of the Bible, this is it. This is the book that deals most openly and directly with all the varying moods and circumstances of our divine-human relationship. One of my colleagues, an Anglican priest named Tory Baucum, has told me of a time early in his Christian walk when he asked his mentor how to pray. "Pray the psalms," his friend replied. "But I don't understand them," Tory objected. "That doesn't matter," his friend said. "They understand you." They do, indeed. Because the psalms encompass the extraordinary range of human emotion and human experience—especially as those experiences affect our relationship with God—they understand us better than if we had written them ourselves.

But who did write them? In a sense, it doesn't matter. Most of us, however, want if possible to know the name of an author. Tradition has helped us in this matter, in that names have been associated with 104 of the 150 psalms. Seventy-four are attributed to David; thus we often refer to this book as "the psalms of David," even though his name is tied to not quite half of the collection. In some instances, we are even told of the circumstances in which David wrote the psalm. As a preacher and teacher, I'm glad for this, because this information helps me in giving human substance to the psalm. But as the Scottish preacher George S. Gunn said, "It is the Psalm itself that is the treasure, not the period or the circumstances in which it was written" (George S. Gunn, *Singers of Israel* [Nashville: Abingdon Press, 1963], 17).

Nevertheless, we enjoy knowing everything we can about those who wrote the psalms. These writers are so candid and transparent that I find myself thinking I've met them somewhere. Twelve of the psalms are attributed to Asaph. Asaph was David's choir director, his in-house musician. His name is attached to one of the most moving and autobiographical of all the psalms, the seventy-third, a poem in which the writer confesses that "my feet had almost stumbled; / my steps had nearly slipped," because he "was envious of the arrogant" when he saw "the prosperity of the wicked" (Psalm 73:2-3). I know, for sure, that I have met Asaph; I've met him in each of the congregations where I was a pastor and several other times along the way.

The "sons of Korah" are identified as the authors of eleven psalms. They represent a story of grace and restoration. In the strenuous days when Moses was leading the nation of Israel through the wilderness, a strong-willed man named Korah mounted a revolt against Moses. On the surface, he sounds like a true populist: "All of the congregation are holy," he said, so why should Moses and Aaron exalt themselves above the rest of the people (Numbers 16:3, adapted)? But I suspect that Korah was more a politician than a populist; he just wanted a piece of the action for himself and the coterie of leaders who had joined him. As the writer of Numbers reports it, the whole group was mercilessly wiped out.

But this was not the end of the story. Ten chapters later the writer reports, "Notwithstanding, the sons of Korah did not die" (Numbers 26:11). Indeed, with the passing of generations, we find them among the hymn writers of Israel. I doubt that these "sons of Korah" were the first generation of Korah's descendants, since the psalms are generally considered from a later era, but we remember that this phrase, "sons of" or "son of," was used to describe any succeeding generations. Thus, kings half-a-dozen generations removed from King David are referred to as a "son of David." But I repeat, there is a message of grace in any psalm that bears the superscription "of the sons of Korah." It is a declaration that no one should be written off because of his or her ancestry. The descendants of a miscreant may some day fill the world with song.

Heman is named as the author of one psalm, Psalm 88. His

name is hardly a household word even among faithful Bible students, but the writer of First Chronicles pays him a fairly lengthy tribute. God had promised "to exalt him; for God had given Heman fourteen sons and three daughters. They were all under the direction of their father for the music in the house of the LORD with cymbals, harps, and lyres for the service of the house of God" (1 Chronicles 25:5-6). Now and then our contemporary culture finds a musical family; I think of several that have been part of television lore over the years. I venture that Heman's seventeen children, all of them singers and some of them also proficient with cymbals, harps, and lyres, would have held their own with any twenty-first-century family combo.

Solomon is named as the author of two psalms, and Ethan and Moses are also credited with a single psalm each. This leaves several psalms for which no author is named; credit them to that well-known personality "Anonymous." I dare to suggest that the forty-six includes both men and women, and persons of widely varying positions and achievements. If Amos, the herdsman, can give us the majestic language of prophecy, who knows what occupations are represented among the nearly a third of the psalms that are unattributed? And if Miriam and Deborah could write songs that are recorded in the Scriptures, why couldn't women be the authors of some of the anonymous psalms?

Let me add a further word about the authorship of the psalms; two comments, in fact. First, this: Biblical scholars raise several questions about the superscriptions that appear with the psalms. The scholars remind us that these entries were not part of the original psalms, and that they probably represent traditions that were attached to particular psalms. We may note, however, that the traditions are very old, and that it is quite likely that the stories on which they are based are very substantial, so we trust them with reason. Second, scholars also remind us that ancient peoples saw authorship differently than we do. After all, there were no copyright laws in those days! When someone entered a superscription such as "A psalm of David," it could mean (as we usually interpret it) "written by David." But it could also mean "in the style of David." Or it could be a poem someone else wrote and dedicated to David; this, too, would be a "psalm of David."

All of this is to say that we shouldn't bet our lives on the authorship of a given psalm, or on the circumstances in which it might have been written. But as I have already said, the traditions surrounding the identified psalms are very old; old enough that the superscriptions are found in the Dead Sea Scrolls (ancient biblical texts that date between the second century B.C. and the first century A.D.), and significant enough that in many versions the verse numbering begins with these notations. So whereas we wouldn't build a doctrine around the authorship or make it an issue of controversy, we can justifiably use the information to help us appreciate the message of the psalm and the mood that seems to infuse the writing. You will find me doing so on occasions in succeeding chapters. But above all, I come back to the basic understanding that the value of a psalm is not in its particular authorship or in the possible peculiar circumstances in which it was written, but in its message.

We discover early that the psalms deal with a vast variety of subjects, but is there any prevailing order in the way the psalms come together? I haven't found any in the years of my reading, and I haven't seen any proof of structure in those scholars who have written about the psalms. There is general agreement that the psalms divide into five books (some feel that this is intended to follow the pattern of the Pentateuch, the first five books of the Bible): Psalms 1–41, Psalms 42–72, Psalms 73–89, Psalms 90–106, and Psalms 107–150. Each of these sections concludes with a statement of finality. It is also true that Psalm 1 is obviously intended to introduce the rest of the collection, and that Psalm 150 is meant to be a grand climax. And there are also several places where psalms of a particular type are clustered together. But on the whole, there is no continuing sense of organization. It's not like a hymnal, where songs are distributed under doctrinal or subject headings, nor is it like any typical modern collection of poetry or readings, where the material is organized topically or chronologically. If you're looking for psalms in a particular mood or covering a particular subject or reflecting a specific period, you will look in vain. The psalmists, and those who finally brought the collection together, seemed to have no such aim in mind. If there is any predictable order, we have yet to discover it.

Perhaps that's the way it should be. The psalms aren't organized, just as friendship isn't organized. We can make ourselves open to friendship, but we can't really make it happen. We can nurture friendship, and we should, but friendship often has a way of confounding us. The friendships that have blessed my life the most beautifully have rarely been predictable. We don't usually give people a Rorschach test for friendship, or a Myers-Briggs. Friendship seems to have some rules of its own, most of which we can never define.

But come to think of it, that shouldn't surprise us, because life isn't neatly organized either, and since friendship unfolds in the context of daily life, it can hardly be expected to fit into neatly engineered rules. Friendship has more to do with desire than with design. It is a grand thing, but it flourishes in common places, and often in unlikely ones, like the flower that blooms through a crack in the asphalt.

And so it is in our friendship with God. It can spring to life anywhere; that's what we mean by *grace*. But having sprung to life, friendship—whether human or divine—deserves attention. The writers of the psalms will teach us how to exercise such attention. We just have to follow the writers as they pursue their own extraordinary friendship with the dearest of all friends: God.

Chapter Two

Secrets of Friendship:
CANDOR

Scripture Reading: Psalm 44

One of the truest measures of friendship is the degree to which we can be candid with one another. Obviously this rule varies with personalities. Some people are candid (perhaps painfully so) with almost everyone, whereas others find it difficult to be candid with even their closest friends. Yet even after qualifying the rule, all of us know how much candor reflects the quality of friendship. At the early stages of friendship, we're guarded in the opinions we venture and careful lest by some ineptness we offend. This carries over into even minor matters. Eating out with someone for the first time, we're likely to be cautious about what we order, wondering if we might in some way offend the other person's taste—and all the more so if the other person is picking up the tab. With an old friend, there is no such uneasiness.

When the friendship is deep and time-tested, we can say whatever is on our minds, even without being unduly careful in our choice of words. We know that the friend will accept our opinion for what it's worth. We know, too, that the friend will look charitably on our sometimes-erratic moods and statements. Later they may remind us playfully about what we said at that unguarded moment, but our irresponsible comments are accepted because we're friends. Friendship makes for candor. And what is true of friendship in general is still truer in the divine-human friendship. No wonder then that candor is such a significant element in the experience of prayer.

I have chosen the words *candor* and *candid* quite deliberately. I might have used the word *honest*, but I have a specific image in mind. I'm thinking of our common expression, "Now let me be candid with you." We use this phrase when we're about to introduce particular honesty into a conversation. Further, I'm using the concept with an eye to our phrase "candid camera" or "a candid shot." One hardly goes to a celebrative kind of social occasion without someone taking pictures at every possible opportunity. If one of these candid shots shows us in questionable light, we're likely to say, defensively, "I don't look like that!" But others reply, "You did when they took the picture. Cameras don't lie." It's no doubt true that we don't always look like we did when the picture was taken—especially, by contrast, when we're able to pose for a picture—but we did look that way when that candid shot was taken.

The book of Psalms is full of candid pictures. It seems never to give us a posed shot. Instead, the psalms show us the writer just as he or she felt at a particular moment. This is one of the loveliest gifts of the book of Psalms. The Bible has preserved for us pictures of the saints in some of their least saintly moments. If I had written some of the psalms, I would have left behind a request: "Please destroy this after I'm gone." But the Scriptures have saved these pictures. We are privileged to see the spiritual giants who wrote the psalms, not in portraits of their spiritual finery, but in the rags of their candid struggles. No wonder, then, that in our own times of despair and struggle, we turn to the book of Psalms. We know we'll find some spiritual kin there.

That's why I think of Psalms as the most candid book in the Bible. That's saying a lot, because the Bible is an altogether candid book. The biblical saints are rarely, if ever, presented in touched-up photographs, and nowhere is this honesty more pronounced than in the psalms. We see the writers' wrinkles and scowls, their sagging jowls and creased brows. Often we sympathize with their complaints, because we see ourselves mirrored in their experience, and we think they have a point. But sometimes their statements are so outrageous that we can only smile and shake our heads in disbelief. When David demands, "Answer me when I call, O God of my right" (Psalm 4:1), we want to say, "Is that any way to talk to God? Indeed, is it any way to talk to *anyone?*" And when in another psalm he asks God to "give heed to my sighing" (Psalm 5:1), any of us who have been exposed to first-rate sighing will agree that this is a bit much to ask of any friend, even of God.

Take Psalm 44. This is what we usually call a "national lament" rather than a personal complaint, but it is full of the candor that so often characterizes the psalms. Quite clearly, it was written during a time when the people of Israel were in disarray. It may have been when they were in captivity or after they had been defeated in battle; in any event, it was a bad time. So the writer begins, as we often do in bad times, by remembering the good old days.

> We have heard with our ears, O God,
>   our ancestors have told us,
> what deeds you performed in their days,
>   in the days of old. (v. 1)

The writer recalls that it was God's own hand that "drove out the nations," and that it was not the power of Israel's armies that brought the victories, "but your right hand, and your arm, / and the light of your countenance, / for you delighted in them" (vv. 2 and 3).

But it's all different now. The writer complains that not

only has God rejected the nation, not only does God not go out with the armies, "You made us turn back from the foe. / ... You have made us like sheep for slaughter, / and have scattered us among the nations. / You have sold your people for a trifle, / demanding no high price for them" (vv. 10-12).

This is a painful report. Only someone whose nation has suffered stunning defeat, or who has gone through some crushing personal defeat or betrayal, can fully empathize with the agony of the writer. But then the psalmist says some things that are so hard to justify that one almost smiles. "All this has come upon us," he says, "yet we have not forgotten you, / or been false to your covenant" (v. 17). Anyone who has read the Hebrew Scriptures knows that if there is any single characteristic that prevails through the entire story it is Israel's repeated periods of unfaithfulness to God. From midway in the book of Exodus all the way through Ezra and Nehemiah, and in most of the writings of the prophets, the story is the same: God is faithful to the covenant, but the people of God are not.

This is one of those points where we understand the psalmist very well. When life is falling apart, we cling to the idea that it shouldn't happen to us. Other people may deserve such ill fortune, but not us! In truth, of course, if we look at ourselves quite objectively, most of us have to say at such times that there's no reason why we should be exempt from common troubles, or even uncommon ones. Such things happen to the rest of the human race, so why not to us? But when we're in trouble, it's hard to make such a confession. Instead, we cling desperately to the idea that we deserve better. The psalmist is making such a case for his nation.

Then he goes a step further: "Rouse yourself! Why do you sleep, O Lord?" (v. 23). A person has to be very sure of the divine friendship to approach God with such insistence. And this is characteristic of the psalmists, whether the psalmist is David, Asaph, a son of Korah, or one of the many anonymous saints. They are so confident of God's friendship, so sure God cares for them unreservedly, that they dare to lay claim to God's mercy and to twist the evidence to prove that they deserve such help. Students of the psalms often note that there are more psalms of lament than any other single kind. If so (and I think the evidence is quite good that it is so), it is high proof of the psalmists' deep conviction that God is a friend to whom one can speak with absolute candor.

In some of this I see what I see as a good synonym for candor. Call it the "just now" mood. In those moments of dramatic honesty, the poet is telling God how he feels at just that moment. He may well get over these feelings an hour from now, or certainly a week, a month, or a year from now. But that isn't the point. The point is that he hurts *just now*, and that's what his prayer is dealing with; not how he will feel when he has had time to think it over and to be philosophical about it and to show proper faith in the ultimate goodness of God. None of these. The issue is *just now*. Just now, he hurts, and hurts deeply. Tell him later that he should have been more patient, and that he should have trusted God. That's all right for later. But just now, it hurts, and he isn't writing later, he's writing just now.

All of us need someone with whom we can be utterly candid. It doesn't matter whether one's life is torn by turmoil or lived in green pastures and beside still waters, we need someone to whom we can say, "Here's how I feel." We ordinarily recognize that need most dramatically when life is difficult, but the need can be equally great in times of ecstasy. The person who has found the love of a lifetime, the parent whose child has won a momentous scholarship, or the couple who has conceived after fearing they would never have a family—all of them need to tell someone. Our psyches demand it. If we try to contain such torrents of emotion, we will damage something about ourselves. Psychosomatically, our digestive system, our blood stream, our heart, and even our joints suffer when we drive our emotions—especially our darker moods—deeply inward. We need an outlet; we need a friend with whom we can be candid.

Most of us, thank God, have some earthly friend who

meets this need in at least a measure. But even the best earthly friends have limits. For one thing, they have troubles of their own. Most of us can remember a time when we planned to tell a close friend some pressing burden of the day, but before we could get out our story, the friend was reciting a plaint of his or her own. I'm happy to report that God has never interrupted my recital of need to say, "You think *you* have troubles? You should try running the universe for a day!"

Also, I like the way God keeps confidences. Even our most trusted friends sometimes forget, and reveal our confidences to someone else. Sometimes they may do so with good intention, as in those instances when they enlist another person to pray for us. Nevertheless, our story has been shared when we intended it to be kept private. I think God is the kind of good Friend who enlists other people to pray for us. I think that's what may be happening on those occasions when someone comes to the mind unbidden; this may be God's nudge to pray for that person. But God reveals no secrets in doing so. God simply enlists us to come alongside a person in need, raising them up by our prayers—prayers of which they may never know, short of eternity.

In the final measure, God is the only Friend with whom we can be utterly and completely honest. Our God is strong enough to hear our complaints, including especially those complaints that may reflect on God's own character. God is never shocked by what we say. God never says, "I wish you hadn't told me that." There is no limit to God's ability to deal with our candor.

Does it seem that perhaps the psalmist has gone beyond the proper boundaries of friendship when he cries, "My God, my God, why have you forsaken me?" (Psalm 22:1)? Is he going too far when he accuses, "O my God, I cry by day, but you do not answer; / and by night, but find no rest" (Psalm 22:2)? This is strong language, no doubt about it, but it is so strong precisely because the psalmist is so confident of God's character. He isn't afraid that God's love is provisional, that it will be withdrawn if we speak anything other than our better thoughts. In a sense, we can pay God no higher compliment than to speak with utter candor. Such honesty reflects the quality of a truly great friendship—a friendship secure enough that we can speak our minds.

But perhaps most important of all, such honesty preserves and enhances friendship. If in a friendship one harbors some ill feeling or some persistent doubt about the other person, a distance comes into the relationship and with it a quality of estrangement. In the summer following her graduation from high school, Joni Eareckson Tada went swimming one bright afternoon, and in a dive hit a rock and became a quadriplegic. A young woman who had been athletic and full of excitement for the future suddenly was so helpless that she couldn't feed herself, couldn't tend to her most personal needs, couldn't even wipe a tear from her eyes. She contemplated suicide but couldn't have brought it about if she had decided to do so, because she couldn't give herself the pills or manipulate the razor.

It was at this point of utter despair that she came to a profoundly deeper relationship with God. She has now lived far more years as a quadriplegic than she had as a girl possessed of all her physical powers, and not only has she become victorious in her own attitude toward life, but through her organization "Joni and Friends" she has become a champion for others who are cruelly disabled.

But it isn't always easy. Those of us in good health sometimes get blue or angry; how much more for someone whose life is so governed by forces outside her control? Some years ago a newspaper reporter asked Joni if she ever got angry with God. She answered, "Sure, I still get angry—if my corset is pinching, or if my arm braces get in the way, or I'm visiting a friend and my catheter suddenly starts to leak all over their couch—sure, I'm angry, I'm humiliated and I want to scream, 'Hey, God, why me?'" But, she says, "I just think it's better to get angry at God, than to walk away from Him" (*The Plain Dealer*, November 11, 1980, p. 3).

This is the wisdom of candor. It is the quality of the ultimate Friendship. And it is the spirit one finds running throughout the psalms. Those remarkable persons who left us the prayers that make up the book of Psalms believed in God so much that they dared to tell God exactly how they felt, even when their feelings were irreverent, doubting, and accusing. It seems implicit that they knew these feelings were transient; beneath the anger was a loving trust that was certain the friendship could stand the kind of ugly stress that expresses itself in nasty words. "Weeping may endure for a night," the psalmist wrote, "but joy comes in the morning" (Psalm 30:5 NKJV). He might also have said, "My God, I am bitterly angry with you just now, but on another day, I will embrace you again." To which God would reply, "Our friendship is good enough to handle times like this."

The sustaining cord of such friendship is candor—absolute honesty with God.

Chapter Three

Secrets of Friendship:
TIME

Scripture Reading: Psalm 1

If you are looking for a fast road to perfection, this chapter is not for you. The main point of what I am about to say is something you've probably heard before, and even if you haven't, you've known its truth instinctively. I hope to approach the issue from a somewhat different angle, but the point itself is an old one. Friendship takes time, and no friendship takes more time than the eternal friendship—the friendship whose manner of relationship is prayer.

I don't need to tell you that friendship is not a matter of rules. As I indicated earlier, friendship comes in a wondrous variety of shapes, sizes, and styles, so it isn't the sort of thing one can program or capture in a formula. Few people are less appealing than those who approach friendship as if it were a geometric formula—which, of course, reduces persons to objects. I do remember, of course, a matter so basic that it goes beyond being a rule; I have no idea of its original source, but I got it from a person who coveted and treasured friendship as much as anyone I've ever known, the late H. Clifford

Northcott, a bishop of The United Methodist Church. "Those who would have friends must show themselves friendly," he often said, and in a sense that's almost all one needs to know about friendship.

The exception is that friendship takes time. It takes time because time is the very expression of love. In its ultimate measure, love causes us to lay down our life for a friend (see John 15:13). It's only rarely that someone pays this ultimate price of friendship, but good friends pay it by the hour, laying down little pieces of their lives by their listening, their attending, their caring. Friendship isn't all high moments and spectacular conviviality; sometimes it's just putting up with the other person, when you'd really rather be free of them. If the ultimate price of friendship is to lay down our lives for another, we can measure friendship in its more mundane forms by the amount of time—that is, in truth, the amount of our lives—we are willing to lay down for someone. Time, I repeat, is the very expression of love.

But friendship also takes time because nothing is as complex and wonderful as a person. Any person. We can't hope to understand something as intricate as another person unless we're willing to invest time in that person. Now and then, as an average friendship grows, we confess that we had at first sold the other person short. We didn't know how much there was to the person; we might even have thought the person was shallow, until we got below the surface. Then we realized the shallowness was not in the other person, but in our own readiness to settle for a skin-deep relationship.

Friendship takes time. This is as true of the divine friendship as of any other. Indeed, even more so, since God has heights, depths, and breadths beyond anything of our imagining or exhausting. The great Hebrew patriarch Abraham is called "the friend of God" (James 2:23). We're not told how he earned this term, but I submit that it was on the basis of the long continuity of his relationship with God. When I read Abraham's story, I am struck by the fact that its intervals are marked by the altars he built. Where some of us trace our biographies by our career changes, or by the births of our children, or by the homes or neighborhoods in which we have lived, Abraham's story is hung on the altars he raised up before God. I see those altars as benchmarks in the steady unfolding of his day-by-day, year-by-year, otherwise quite ordinary friendship.

But I repeat, most of us have always known, usually to our discomfort, that we ought to pray more. Common sense says so, and so does a nagging conscience or a pestering pulpit. But how do the psalms teach us the importance of time? They never sermonize to that end, nor do they at any time instruct us to pray a certain number of hours.

If I may say so, the point is more subtly made. It is written into the very nature and structure of Hebrew poetry. The psalms simply make it impossible for us to hurry by forcing us to repeat ourselves; and the peculiar nature of the repeating compels us to think, even as we repeat what we have just said.

Let me tell you what I mean. Most of the poetry we know best depends upon rhythm and also, frequently, on rhyme. When my sixth-grade Sunday-school teacher told us that the psalms were poetry, I remember feeling a bit sorry for her, because she didn't know what poetry was. I knew about poetry; it was pretty well symbolized by the lovely rhythm and rhyme of "I think that I shall never see / A poem lovely as a tree" (Joyce Kilmer, "Trees"). I saw none of that in the psalms, especially in the only Bible available to us in my childhood, the King James Version. The verses were not set up in the form of poetry, and nothing rhymed, so how could it be poetry?

Interestingly enough, it wasn't until the end of the eighteenth century that biblical scholars themselves recognized that the psalms (and also most of the rest of the Old Testament Wisdom literature, as well as a great deal of the prophets) were written as poetry. The problem was in the limited way scholars had defined poetry. In looking so insistently for the usual elements of rhyme and rhythm, they looked right past the unique structural beauty of the psalms, the structure of repetition. But it was not meaningless repetition. To the contrary, the repetition was very carefully organized, to the point that sometimes the psalmist seemed a kind of literary architect, putting together a linguistic house.

Robert Lowth, an eighteenth-century professor of poetry at Oxford University, used the term *parallelism* to describe the style of the Hebrew poets, a style that also characterized other poetry of the ancient Middle East. I think it could be said that where our poetry often rhymes words, this poetry "rhymed" *ideas*. So the first line or part of a line declares a point, and the second line (and sometimes a third or fourth) reinforces it. Lowth noted that this parallelism usually showed itself in one of three ways: *synonymous, antithetic,* and *synthetic.*

Take Psalm 1. The first verse is a perfect example of the *synonymous,* where the succeeding line or lines say the same thing as the first but in different words or employing a different metaphor—just as we choose between several adjectives, adverbs, or verbs that are synonymous, searching for the one that serves our insight best. Listen to this verse in the familiar rhythm of the King James Version, but set up in a way that emphasizes the parallelism:

> Blessed is the man
> that walketh not in the counsel of the ungodly,
> nor standeth in the way of sinners,
> nor sitteth in the seat of the scornful.

The message in all three lines is the same: Avoid the influence of wicked persons. The poet's point is clear in the first line, and the second and third lines simply reinforce the point with synonyms, so to speak. And in this case not only are the lines synonymous, the poet also makes parallels within the lines: in the verb (*walketh, standeth, sitteth*), the place of action (*counsel, way, seat*), and the perpetrator (*ungodly, sinners, scornful*).

Psalm 1 gives us an equally impressive example of the *antithetic* type of parallel. In this form, the poet makes a point by way of contrast, lines in which he states a thesis and then an antithesis. So we have:

> For the LORD knoweth the way of the righteous;
> but the way of the ungodly shall perish. (v. 6, KJV)

When I write those lines I want instinctively to follow the first line with an arrow that goes up, and the second line with an arrow that goes down. But the two lines are making the same point, that it's better to be righteous. They make the point, however, not by synonym but by contrast. This form, incidentally, appears a great deal in the book of Proverbs, where good and bad conduct or wise and stupid conduct are contrasted.

In *synthetic* lines, the second line completes the thought of the first. So, in Psalm 1, "And he shall be like a tree planted by the rivers of water, / that bringeth forth his fruit in his season" (v. 3, KJV). Personally, I like the term *sequential* for this type of parallel, because it seems to me that this describes more clearly what is happening: The second or third line is part of a sequence of thought. But I suspect I have chosen a simpler word in not fully appreciating all that Robert Lowth had in mind.

Do you see what parallelism does? It simply won't let us hurry. As the late Mary Ellen Chase said, "To [the psalmists], once is not enough. They must say twice what they long to say, or three times, or even four in a succession of often tumultuous lines" (Mary Ellen Chase, *The Psalms for the Common Reader* [New York: W. W. Norton & Company, 1962], 74). Dietrich Bonhoeffer, the martyr-theologian who died under Adolf Hitler, insisted that the parallelism was "not simply accidental. It encourages us not to allow the prayer to be cut off prematurely." Bonhoeffer continued, "That which seems to be unnecessary repetition to us, who are inclined to pray too hurriedly, is actually proper

immersion and concentration in prayer" (Dietrich
Bonhoeffer [translated by James H. Burtness], *Psalms: The
Prayer Book of the Bible* [Minneapolis: Augsburg Publishing
House, 1970], 24).

I take some strange comfort in Bonhoeffer's saying that we
"are inclined to pray too hurriedly." Then it is not simply our
speed-ridden, computer-driven, instant-satisfaction culture
that can't find time to pray, or that seeks quick-fix spiritu-
ality; Bonhoeffer dealt with the same problem sixty or sev-
enty years ago. And come to think of it, perhaps the saintliest
souls of twenty-five or thirty centuries ago recognized the
same human tendency. Whatever the style of the Hebrew
poets, they were wise to use such structures when they
prayed.

In truth, I suspect that every generation of humans has had
to be encouraged to "take time to be holy." After all,
although communing with God can be magnificently real, it
is also, most of the time, very intangible. You and I know
when we have cooked a meal, written a contract, or attended
a concert; these are things we can see and measure, and often
touch. Talking with God is not so visible and tangible. We
know when we have finished cooking the soup, but we don't
often know when we have completed God's purpose in our
prayers. We know, too, that it's important to pray; great
souls throughout the ages have told us so, and our own
hearts know it beyond argument when there is a 9/11 or a
shattering tsunami.

And yet, we find it difficult to take time to pray. If the
liturgy of our church seems overly long, we shift nervously
on our knees or in our seat. If we have set aside fifteen minutes for private prayer, we're likely to begin checking our
wristwatch after seven or eight minutes. We want to pray,
and we know we should, but there's work to be done, there
are telephone calls to be made, and there is e-mail to be
answered. Or even less nobly, there is a sports section to be
read, or a soap opera to be watched, or a news special to
attend to. Who has time to *pray*?

And to this the ancient poet says, "You do, and I do." But we have to be compelled to. Perhaps we would do better at finding the time if prayer arrived at our doorstep each morning, like the newspaper, or if we had to tune it in at a stated hour. As a matter of fact, those who pray best are those who schedule prayer into their day the way they schedule everything else that is important. I believe in Paul's admonition to "pray without ceasing" (1 Thessalonians 5:17), and I seek in my uneven way to fulfill his counsel. But I have learned—as perhaps you have, too—that I'm more likely to pray on the run and in the midst of other pursuits when I have set aside an earlier time to devote myself entirely to prayer. Friendship takes time, and in no friendship is time more crucial than in the divine friendship, where the means of communication is prayer.

The psalmists didn't lecture about time with God, they simply implemented it. Is there something to be said to God? Then say it—not once, but twice or three times. And don't say it the same way each time to do so would be to engage in the "vain repetitions" or "empty phrases" that Jesus warned against (Matthew 6:7 KJV, NRSV). Such praying becomes lazy; the brain is put in an idling mode, and the words roll out without thought or content. The psalmist would have none of that. He speaks his heart to God, and then searches for a way to say it again. Having rejoiced in a God who "makes me lie down in green pastures," he follows his metaphor a step further: "he leads me beside still waters" (Psalm 23:2).

This kind of praying requires attentiveness. I confess that I long for such mental involvement when I hear an extemporaneous prayer that seems made up almost entirely of "just" and repeated uses of the name of God; or when I hear someone read a written prayer with so little emphasis or meaning that I fear the thought hasn't gone below the first level. I repeat, the psalmists would have nothing to do with such praying. They honored the divine friendship by taking the time to speak in a way that involved both heart and mind, and blood and intelligence. Even in the most passionate outpourings, when the psalmist sensed he or she was on the edge of a precipice, there was still the involvement of the whole person.

Samuel Johnson is known to students of literature as a landmark figure, as a lexicographer, an essayist, a biographer, and a poet. But a vast number of people, at a variety of levels, knew him as a friend. Indeed, Johnson often repented that his capacity for conversation interfered with his literary responsibilities. But he knew the value of friendship. "A man, Sir," he said to his friend James Boswell, "should keep his friendship in constant repair." So it is with our divine friendship. And that takes time.

Several years ago I was a guest preacher for several nights at a church in Paducah, Kentucky. One evening the pastor spotted a visiting layperson in the congregation and left the ritual of the evening to ask the man to offer the evening prayer. He had spoken only a sentence or two before I recognized that this man who was unknown to me was well known to God. He stepped naturally and reverently into the King's presence, and I followed him, as did most of the congregation, I'm sure, with gratitude. He and God were on the kind of friendship terms that made preliminaries unnecessary. Obviously, they had talked often enough in the past that this occasion of public prayer simply took up where their last visit had left off.

That kind of friendship requires time. The psalmists understood that. They didn't talk about or give rules for it; they simply wrote it into the structure of their prayers. It takes time to be holy, and to have a holy friendship.

Chapter Four

Secrets of Friendship:
BEAUTY

Scripture Reading: Psalm 119

I had read the psalms, loved the psalms, and lived with the psalms for years before I realized the importance of their beauty. I recognized the beauty and enjoyed it; I simply didn't appreciate its importance—perhaps because I was taking the beauty for granted. Then, too, I suspect I didn't recognize the importance of beauty's role in worship in those days. It was certainly not a dominant factor in our house of worship or in the worship itself. The churches in which I spent my childhood and youth were modest, indeed. So, too, was the music. The soloists were earnest but limited, and the most ambitious choir anthem was "The Awakening Chorus," which was memorable more for its vigor than for excellence of production. The times were hard financially, and adornments in life were few. Perhaps here was a difference between Protestantism and Catholicism. A Catholic church in even the poorest community was likely to have a certain stateliness and glamour, but our Protestant churches tended to reflect our neighborhoods and our way of life.

As for prayer, the emphasis in my little world (which, I learned later, was a fairly representative one) was on spontaneity and sincerity, not eloquence. We had heard, in our small Methodist church, that in some larger churches the pastor wrote the prayer that was offered on Sunday morning, and we found this highly suspect. Was it because the pastor was so unaccustomed to prayer that he wouldn't know what to say if there was no manuscript before him? We thought such prayers pretentious. Somehow it never occurred to us that the psalms we cherished so much were prayers, were written for our continuing use, and were beautiful; beautiful, indeed, with the kind of beauty that rarely can happen except as someone invests time and effort in the quest for loveliness.

But there's another question before I go further, since the motif of this book is friendship. How is beauty an issue in the care and growth of friendship? Friendship is itself beautiful, but we don't think of friendship as something that demands beauty. To the contrary, friendship is a comfortable thing. One of the elements of friendship that appeals to us so much is the ease we feel when we're with a friend; the better the friendship, the higher the comfort level. When we join a friend after a business or professional gathering, we're likely to say, "It's so nice to be able to relax and just be myself." This seems sometimes to be almost the essence of friendship. As the saying has it, we don't have to put on any airs, and we don't have to impress, we can just be ourselves. And certainly that's one of the friendship qualities in prayer, too; I was saying as much in the chapter on candor.

So what does beauty have to do with friendship, whether the friendship is with earthly companions or with God? Actually, a very great deal. Because while friendship makes us so comfortable that it sometimes seems nothing is required of us, at the same time friendship makes us extend ourselves for the sake of the friend. Your friend likes this eatery on the other side of town, a location somewhat inconvenient for you? No matter, you'll go there. You remember that a certain day is special for your friend (who may also be your parent, your spouse, your sibling, or your child); with that in mind, you write a note or an e-mail in celebration, or perhaps even send or deliver some remembrance. Different people express this "beauty" in different ways. I note that many women are likely to put forth particular effort for a beautiful table if they're inviting a close friend for lunch. A man who might laugh at the idea of treating his buddy with beauty will try to surprise his friend by getting tickets in the stadium section his friend likes best. Because friendship itself is beautiful, our inclination is to celebrate its beauty by some deed or word of beauty.

Sadly, friendship can also take an unfortunate turn. It's very easy to take friendship so for granted that we presume on it. Instead of rewarding friendship with beauty, we can desecrate it by indifference. If we discover that we are more attentive to a near stranger whose favor we court than to a friend or spouse of whose loyalty we are sure, we should recognize that our conduct is blaspheming friendship.

I think it's even easier to presume on the divine friendship. This may well be our most besetting sin. The more we experience of the goodness of God, the more we are in danger of the ingratitude that neglects the source of that goodness. In any friendship, human or divine, we need to pause at frequent intervals and ask ourselves if we have allowed favor to make us presumptuous. Without being morbid, we should pause to ask, "What would my life be like without this friendship?" And then, we should seek to celebrate the wonder of friendship with some act of beauty.

The psalmist was constantly about this business of bringing beauty into the divine friendship. The prayers of the psalms are such passionate, heartfelt, tumultuous writings, yet their dominant characteristic is beauty. This beauty seems appropriate when the prayer is one of adoration or thanksgiving. But there seems to be the same quest for beauty when the writer is bereft in the midst of trouble, or bitterly angry at what he or she feels is God's neglect or indifference. Still we have the measured lines, the careful balance of phrases, sometimes the intricate play on words.

Psalm 119, which is both the longest psalm and the longest chapter in the Bible, is a particularly good example of the psalmist's commitment to beauty. C. S. Lewis described it as "a pattern, a thing done like embroidery, stitch by stitch, through long, quiet hours, for love of the subject and for the delight in leisurely, disciplined craftsmanship" (C. S. Lewis, *Reflections on the Psalms* [London: Geoffrey Bles, 1958], 58-59). I like Lewis's comparison with embroidery, because it seems to me that there's a sense in which this poem is more like some handicraft—embroidery, needlework, or cabinet-making—than like a painting. It doesn't have the flashes of ecstatic beauty we find in the work of poet Gerard Manley Hopkins, for instance; rather, it is the kind of work that makes a person step back after a while and say, "Now, isn't that nice!"

This psalm invests all of its 176 verses in praise of the Law of the Lord. In all but four of these verses, it includes a word for the law—*statutes, commandments, judgments, promise, precepts, decrees,* for instance. The psalm is written as an alphabetic acrostic, with twenty-two stanzas of eight verses each, and within each stanza each verse begins with the given letter of the Hebrew alphabet. Thus the first eight verses each begin with A*leph,* the next eight verses with B*eth,* then G*imel,* and so on through the twenty-two letters of the entire Hebrew alphabet. I repeat, it's like a work of needlepoint. Lewis says that we "can guess at once" that the writer "felt about the Law somewhat as he felt about his poetry; both involved exact and loving conformity to an intricate pattern" (Lewis, *Reflections,* p. 59).

For the person who wrote this psalm, it was obviously an act of love, a work of holy friendship. He or she wanted it to be something beautiful for God, something worthy of its subject matter, the Law of the Lord. I wonder if perhaps this psalm was the work of a committee, like the King James translation of the Bible. It's not impossible, and neither does such an idea diminish for me the quality of divine inspiration. As a parish pastor and seminary professor I have lived long enough with committees to see them with a cautious eye, but I have found that the Holy Spirit can work through committees, as indeed the Spirit did in the grand King James Version; perhaps it was also the case with this lengthy psalm.

But whoever the author or authors, this psalm, like all the rest, majors in beauty. It is clear that the writers of the psalms meant for their prayers to be worthy of the God they were addressing. They knew that God accepts us just as we are. They appealed to God to hear their "sighing," which is surely one of the less eloquent forms of communication. On another occasion the psalmist says confidently, "You have kept count of my tossings; / put my tears in your bottle. / Are they not in your record?" (Psalm 56:8). All of which indicates that these saintly folk believed God accepted every manner of prayer. Nevertheless, they aimed in their prayer book to craft objects of beauty.

But another question arises. *Should* prayers be beautiful? Granted, the psalms are works of art, but "they're different"; isn't it likely that in writing a beautiful prayer we become more absorbed with ourselves and our artistry, to a point where God is secondary? And isn't it likely that a certain artificiality or phoniness comes into prayer when we become so engrossed in finding just the right word? Eliza Doolittle, in *My Fair Lady,* objects that she's "so sick of words . . . just *show* me." I'm sure something of that feeling enters the minds of those who take prayer very seriously and who feel that its passion is somehow diluted if the prayer is written.

I mentioned earlier that in the little church of my childhood we were suspicious of a written pastoral prayer. I find now that this was not unique to our modest congregation. John H. Leith notes in his study of doctrine that although John Calvin used both extemporaneous and written prayers, many of his later followers in the Presbyterian tradition would "protest against read prayer, a protest that was alive in the Presbyterian church until after the Second World War." The concern in the Puritan tradition was that "prayer must come from the heart" (John H. Leith, *Basic Christian*

Doctrine [Louisville: Westminster/John Knox Press, 1993], 266).

Without a doubt, that heart quality is in danger in a written prayer. I will dare to say (though those who believe deeply in the inspiration of the Scriptures, as I do, may be uncomfortable with my saying so) that I wonder if the writers of the psalms sometimes teetered at this place where the artist and the saint are at possible odds. A person beloved may find great pleasure in the language of her lover, but if the lover seems more taken with his language than with the object of his love, the language becomes distasteful. That is, language should be a means to an end, not the end in itself—and never more so than in worship.

The point at which this issue is most significant is, of course, in public prayer. It can be very easy to write or speak a prayer with the wrong audience in mind. Prayer is to God, not to the body of persons gathered. This can be difficult to remember when one is praying for a public occasion, such as the inauguration of a public official or the ceremonial prayer at a banquet or a school commencement. To write a prayer with the intention of impressing the human audience is a kind of blasphemy—and yet, a tempting one.

The problem is made more complicated by the reality of a phrase we often use at times of public prayers: "*lead* in prayer." A person who prays before a body, while speaking to God, is also speaking *for* an assembled body. Their participation in the prayer depends partly upon the skill with which the appointed person leads. The leader should therefore choose words carefully, to make it as easy as possible for the "followers" to engage themselves in both the content and the spirit of the prayer. If the person leading in prayer is elevated in both language and heart, the congregation is far more likely to find themselves lifted toward God.

But the aim of the beauty must be God. There is the issue. It is very simple, but not always easy to remember. We seek for beauty of language because we want to give pleasure to God. We will not understand this if we think of prayer simply as a means of getting things. We will understand it best if prayer becomes the language of friendship, and if our friendship reaches a point where nothing matters to us as much as that the friendship be as nearly mutual as a divine-human friendship can be; and since God has given us so much pleasure by the abundance of divine beauty, we want to return the kindness by giving pleasure to God.

Can our simple, often fumbling and generally inadequate efforts bring pleasure to God? Without a doubt, if God is indeed our heavenly parent. If earthly parents find so much satisfaction in a crayon picture that we place it on the refrigerator door or under the glass on an executive desk, is not God pleased when we seek just the right word or deed in our communication? And if our earnest effort reflects our love for God, then surely God responds to that beauty.

I don't think the writers of the psalms always prayed with such eloquent phrases; the references to sighs and tears indicate otherwise. But sometimes they wrote beauty into their prayers, and we are now the beneficiaries of that search for loveliness.

So although I grew up with prayers that had little form or comeliness, I now seek at times to bring together my best for my Lord. I still do not write my public prayers; some things in a boy remain with him even as an older man. But I think through those prayers. And more than that: Each morning, as part of my communion with God, I write a prayer. It isn't the sort of thing that would ever go into a collection of prayers, but it represents my taking time enough to put words on paper, as an act of love for God. And if I'm asked on the spur of the moment to offer prayer at lunch or at a Rotary Club meeting, I will first breathe a quick, silent prayer that I may find words that are just right—simple though the theme may be—for this occasion: words that will *lead* those who are with me, and words that will have some small tincture of beauty for the God whom I adore.

And there is still more. I remember the ancient word: "Our prayer is the work of our hands." Here is a goal for every

Christian. Paul Johnson, the English historian and essayist, says, "God is the greatest of all connoisseurs." Johnson notes that so many great artists, architects, poets, and composers have sought to produce work that glorified God (Paul Johnson, *The Quest for God* [New York: HarperCollins, 1996], 78-80). Anton Bruckner, for example, dedicated his last and greatest symphony "To Almighty God," and Johann Sebastian Bach signed nearly every piece of his work "To the glory of God alone."

I'm quite sure I'm naively hopeful, but I wish that all of us, as Christians, would go about our days in such a spirit. I see a gardener, pausing at the end of a row of weeding, looking upon the clean line as an offering to God. I want someone to set the table for a dinner party, not simply to favor the guests, but to please God. I would like for that lover of needlepoint to hold up the finished product and ask God to enjoy its beauty. I long for a taxi driver (and there are such) who delivers me to the airport with a sense of holy pleasure at having made his way through the streets with order and efficiency.

The psalmists would understand what I'm trying to say. They brought to God the disparate pieces of life, many of them ugly or mundane in themselves, and wrapped them in such love and beauty that still today, many centuries later, we bask in their beauty as well as in their reverence. They intended to do something beautiful for God. I am simple enough to believe that God finds pleasure in all such doing.

Chapter Five

Secrets of Friendship:
PLACE, POSTURE, AND PUNCTUALITY

*Scripture Reading: Selected passages—Psalms 5:7;
6:6; 42:8; 63:4, 6; 84:1-4; 108:2; 119:62, 164;
122:1-2; 123:1; 1 Thessalonians 5:17*

The title of this chapter may seem to have little to do with friendship as we know it today. "Place, posture, and punctuality" suggests a world where one presented a calling card to a servant or another member of the family before being admitted to see the desired person—and after being admitted, sitting properly in a stiff chair until one sensed the appointed time had come for the meeting to end.

I'm sorry if my words paint such a picture. I confess that my title can easily reflect the style and structure of another day. And to a degree, I'm not sorry about that. Because whereas friendship has too many spontaneous qualities to be forced into a preordered mold, it deserves and demands certain structures. Other generations probably employed social structures more consciously in the nurture of friendship. We don't have so many acknowledged rules, because we are just now an aggressively informal age. Nevertheless, we have some rules. We practice them instinctively, because in truth, friendship must have a context if it is to flourish, and this context involves place and punctuality for certain, and posture more than we realize.

Take the matter of *place*. After a time, friends tend to meet at the same place for lunch or coffee, sometimes even the same booth. If you go to Oxford, England, you'll find a certain pub, and in it a certain booth, where the Inklings—C. S. Lewis, Charles Williams, J. R. R. Tolkien, and others of their small circle—met regularly. The booth is now marked in their memory; the Inklings marked it long before, in friendship. If you and a friend meet in your homes, you soon gravitate to the same chairs. Friendship likes order, perhaps because order adds to the sense of security that characterizes friendship.

So, too, with *punctuality*, by which I mean having a somewhat regular time for meeting. I concede readily that a good friendship is good at all times, but friendship is usually nurtured by certain patterns of regularity. High-school friends meet between stated classes, and neighbors meet at a particular time of the day or week. Walkers or joggers who follow a faithful regimen expect after a while to pass another person at a given spot. The two may never know each other's names, but they find a peculiar friendship-in-passing simply because they're on the same schedule in the same place, and if one of them misses a morning, the other is peculiarly concerned.

As for *posture*, we're probably glad that social convention no longer demands that we sit in a prescribed way; again, we're at an informal juncture in history. Nevertheless, we pay attention to the posture of a friend. If a friend seems poised on the edge of a chair, we challenge them: "What's wrong? Are you in a hurry?" We want a friend to be relaxed, but if they seem unduly relaxed we may be upset that they aren't really concerned about what we're saying. The other person's body language influences the flow, the quality, and the depth of conversation.

So what about prayer? Do the psalms teach us anything

about place, posture, and punctuality? Again, the psalms offer no set rules. The psalmists never tell us that we must pray at a certain place or time, in a particular body position. But they give us a wonderful variety of examples from which we can learn.

Let's begin with posture. This aspect of prayer would have called for little discussion in my father's day, or your grandparents' day. My father had postures of prayer, and they were taken for granted. He knelt beside his bed at night; I suspect he would have thought it pagan if someone had suggested that he could say his evening prayers in bed. In our little church, we stood for what might be called the pastoral prayer or the service prayer. I remember well the associate minister, an older man who seldom preached but whose prayers, it was commonly complained, went to sermonic lengths. It was a long time standing when he led the way, but stand we did, because that was the proper posture for such a prayer. In churches in the Catholic and Anglican traditions, the times of prayer are times of kneeling, and the regular communicants know when to slip to their knees. So, too, to pray in many Holiness and Pentecostal congregations means to go to one's knees, though probably by a complete reposturing of the body at the pew or chair where one is sitting.

Does the posture matter? Blaise Pascal, a devout believer and one of the truly great minds of human history, reasoned that it did. In *Pensées* he wrote, "The external must be joined to the internal to obtain anything from God, that is to say, we must kneel, pray with the lips, etc., in order that proud man, who would not submit himself to God, may now be subject to the creature. To expect help from these externals is superstition; to refuse to join them to the internal is pride." Pascal's distinction is a penetrating one. Thinking that our posture wins favor with God or that it ensures an answer to prayer reduces prayer to magic; however, if we refuse to place ourselves under some particular, reasonable physical discipline, our pride can separate us from God.

But what do the psalmists say? In one instance, "I will *bow down*" (Psalm 5:7, emphasis added). But by contrast, "When I think of you *on my bed*" (Psalm 63:6, emphasis added). We see this person with head tilted back: "To you I *lift up my eyes*" (Psalm 123:1, emphasis added), and on another occasion with the whole body involved in prayer: "I will *lift up my hands* and call on your name" (Psalm 63:4, emphasis added).

Obviously, these verses indicate a good deal of variety in posture. Does this mean, then, that posture didn't matter to these ancient saints? To the contrary, the verses indicate that posture mattered a very great deal; this is why the writer bothers to mention it. Clearly, the several writers were associating particular postures and bodily actions with their prayers. That is, the posture was an aid to the specific mood of the prayer. See for yourself how the mood changes as the posture changes. Sit and pray, and prayer takes on a conversational quality. Stand, and you feel you are making an appearance before the King. Lift your hands, and a special sense of adoration engulfs your prayer. Put your head down, and you feel awe, humility, perhaps even shame; lift your head, and there is a sense of glad openness, to a point where unconsciously you may smile.

All of which is to say that the great saints of the book of Psalms did not recommend a single posture, but by their action they emphasized the importance of posture. Which posture? The one that best fits the mood you feel, or perhaps the mood you *ought* to feel.

I do not consider myself an example to be followed, though I have been privileged over a fairly long lifetime to be near some very godly people, both known and unknown. I'm sure that everything I tell you about prayer reflects something of these many associations. But let me dare to say what has happened in my own life. As a boy, to pray earnestly meant to go to my knees. Early in my pastoral ministry, I formed the habit of conducting my personal morning prayers sitting in a chair; I even put the concept into a sermon that I titled "God Is in the Next Chair." On occasions of great distress, I have lain prostrate on the floor to pray. I enjoy praying while walking. I commend any and all of these possibilities to you. But in the past year, I have gained new appreciation for the pattern of my childhood. Now, nearly every morning, I go to my knees before God. I find that the position is good for my soul. Physically, it reminds me that God is God and I am not.

The ancient saints, those persons who gave us the psalms, knew that posture matters. Centuries before there was a "science" of body language, they understood the body language of the spirit. I repeat, they didn't insist on one particular posture of prayer, but they testified by their practice that posture matters. The wrong posture for a given occasion can impede prayer, whereas the right posture aids us in our reach to God.

And what of the *place* to pray? When the apostle Paul urged believers to "pray without ceasing" (1 Thessalonians 5:17), he seemed to recommend making the whole world our altar. That's certainly not a bad idea. But are some places better than others? The psalmist said as much when he exulted, "I was glad when they said to me, / 'Let us go to the house of the Lord!'" (Psalm 122:1). Very clearly, he thought of God's house as a special place. His second line affirmed the conviction: "Our feet are standing / within your gates, O Jerusalem." Surely Jerusalem and the temple are the place to be. You have the same feeling when a psalmist writes, "I will bow down toward your holy temple / in awe of you" (Psalm 5:7).

But nowhere do the Hebrew saints make the point more emphatically and more beautifully than in Psalm 84:

> How lovely is your dwelling place,
>   O Lord of hosts!
> My soul longs, indeed it faints
>   for the courts of the Lord;
> my heart and my flesh sing for joy
>   to the living God (vv. 1-2)

This house of worship is a place so lovely that "the sparrow finds a home" there, and the swallow finds not only

45

"a nest for herself," but even a place "where she may lay her young" (Psalm 84:3). No wonder, then, "Happy are those who live in your house, / ever singing your praise" (Psalm 84:4).

So is a *church*—to move the Old Testament writer into our world—the best place to pray? In truth, there *is* something special about a church as a place to pray. Quite simply, when a building or a place is dedicated to a particular purpose, it takes on unique qualities of that purpose. When I am the guest preacher in a church, I sometimes invite people to come to the altar for prayer with a reminder that although they can pray anywhere, there is something special about praying at the altar of a church. Why? Because not only has the altar been dedicated to the purpose of prayer and holy adoration, it has taken on the hallowedness of the many prayers that have been offered there. I confess that I am somewhat mystical about this; a place where many have prayed has an aura of its own.

But of course we can pray anywhere. The psalmist spoke of thinking of God on "my bed" (Psalm 63:6), and of "flood[ing] my bed with tears" and "my couch with weeping" (Psalm 6:6), and all in the spirit of intense prayer. Several people are credited with a line that was famous during World War II: "There are no atheists in foxholes." It was a tribute to the fact that in life's direst circumstances, the place of near-hopelessness becomes a shrine of faith. Many of us have built such a temporary altar in the intensive-care unit of a hospital, or at the bedside of a hospice center.

For day-by-day piety, however, or when building a consistent devotional life, I recommend establishing some set place for daily communion with God. If you're fortunate, it can be a particular room. For me, it is a particular chair where I sit to read my Bible and devotional literature, and where I kneel to pray. Some clergy have a *prie-dieu,* a type of kneeling bench for use in prayer, in their study; and I doubt not that some devout laypersons have purchased such an item for their homes. We add to the strength of such a spot if there is room for a Bible and a prayer book or aid. In my prayer area, I am blessed by a certain picture that draws me to Calvary. I know some who keep a small plant or fresh flowers at their place of prayer. These physical elements can nurture the uncertain, trembling faith we bring to our prayer time.

Amy Carmichael, the remarkable missionary to India, and surely a saint, loved to recall her earliest prayer setting. As a tiny child, just after the nursery light had been turned low and she was "quite alone," she would "smooth a little place on the sheet, and say aloud, but softly, to our Father, 'Please come and sit with me.'" Late in her life she testified that this "baby custom" blessed her still (Stuart and Brenda Blanch, *Learning of God: Readings from Amy Carmichael* [London: Triangle SPCK, 1985], 3).

So how do the psalms guide us regarding the place of prayer? They emphasize, surely, the wonder of the house of worship, and so should we. But they also make clear, by their practice, that any place can become sacred space. The secret is not location, but the attitude of the heart. Because of our psychological makeup, we do well to establish some given spot, whether in our home, our church, or a walking path. It's important also that we mark that place by regularity and frequency. A prayer spot, no matter how sacred of itself, will soon lose its power if it is visited only rarely.

And then there's the matter of *punctuality*. Does it matter *when* we pray? Again, the psalmists give us several answers. If you have studied the practices of the saints, you won't be surprised that the psalmist says, "I will awake the dawn" (Psalm 108:2). There's no encouragement here for the slugabed! Even those who insist that they are "night people" must confess that how we start the day is important. Saint Francis de Sales called morning "the best part of the day," and he told those he mentored that they should retire early enough to wake up early in the morning. "Early rising is good for health and holiness," he said.

But what if your way of life is all against such a practice? Suppose you work the third shift; in such a case, morning prayer-time is go-to-bed time. And what if your family responsibilities make it impossible for you to have time alone first thing in the day? Is early morning the only really good time for prayer?

Our ancient Hebrew saints found a variety of sacred hours. "By day the LORD commands his steadfast love, / and at night his song is with me" (Psalm 42:8). Perhaps it was a night person who wrote, "At midnight I rise to praise you" (Psalm 119:62), or perhaps his sense of gratitude was so insistent that sleep fled from him. At another point a psalmist takes command of the whole day for God: "Seven times a day I praise you" (Psalm 119:164). To the Hebrews, seven was the number of completeness or perfection, so no doubt this writer was saying not simply that the day was marked by seven occasions of prayer, but that prayer filled the day and completed it. In a sense the ancient writer was saying what the apostle Paul said when he called for prayer "without ceasing."

So is there a "right" time for prayer? The psalmists would endorse morning, noon, night, any hour, every hour. Saints in the Christian tradition would reinforce the idea that any time is an appropriate time for prayer; and most of them would also emphasize the importance of prayer early in the day—a logic which, even if unattractive to some, is hard to deny.

What, then, do we conclude about the formalities of prayer, as these ancient saints practiced it? I think it's very clear that time, place, and posture all matter. They matter differently at different times, for different reasons. They are not determinative in power, so we shouldn't become superstitious about a particular place or posture or practice; but they can enhance our effectiveness in prayer. Since you and I are human creatures, our human circumstances affect even our spiritual moments—including especially the moments of friendship, both human and divine.

But whatever the formalities of time, place, and posture, the psalmists would tell us, as would centuries of saints since their time, "Pray. Just pray!"

Chapter Six

Secrets of Friendship:
EXUBERANCE

Scripture Reading: Psalms 96 and 98

Exuberance, my dictionary says, is "the state of being exuberant"; and *exuberant,* in turn, is defined as "effusively and almost uninhibitedly enthusiastic," with the explanation including such other words as "luxuriant" and "superabundant." You get the idea. The word comes to us from the world of nature: *uber* means "fertile," and "exuber" conveys the sense of fruitfulness and abundance. It's the feeling people had when all of us lived close to nature, and a farmer and his family looked out on a field or vineyard nearly ready for harvest and exulted in the prospects: No starvation this year, but plenty! *Exuberance!*

Friendship has its times of exuberance. Not all the time, of course; those who want only exuberance in friendship are looking not for friendship but for entertainment and diversion. Friendship is too substantial a thing to be composed only of dancing and laughter; but just as surely, a quality of overflow and abundance is woven all through friendship. Thus even when friendship suffers the pain of loss or of separation, the language dealing with the loss can sometimes slip over easily into laughter. I suspect that's why conversations after a funeral so often slip into humorous anecdotes. Only in the most tragic of deaths is this quality missing, and sometimes it intervenes even then.

Exuberance! Our literature of friendship is full of it. This is the stuff out of which we write and sing school songs. It is the trademark of New Year's Eve, when everyone breaks into "Auld Lang Syne." All those sentimental ballads about mother, father, and other kin celebrate the specialized forms of friendship we enjoy in the family and in the fruitfulness of life—the exuberance—they provide. Sometimes literature's exuberance in friendship is in a distinctly minor key, when death has intervened. David says when he learns of the death of his cherished friend, Jonathan, "I am distressed for you, my brother Jonathan; / greatly beloved were you to me" (2 Samuel 1:26); and in modern times, W. H. Auden says at the death of a friend, "He was my North, my South, my East and West" (W. H. Auden, "Funeral Blues"). The language is grief-stricken, yet in its own way exuberant, in that it is language that is strained to the limit to pay tribute to the wonder of friendship. Sometimes, words are not enough. Perhaps the exuberance of friendship is never more eloquent than at those times when we replace words with an embrace, whether of reunion or of farewell.

I submit that this exuberance of friendship reaches its most ecstatic expression when the book of Psalms celebrates the divine-human friendship. When I tried to choose an appropriate scripture for this chapter, I found I was overwhelmed by abundance. It's not simply that the psalmists are grateful for God's care or adoring of God's character; it is the utterly unrestrained language in which they express these feelings. Even those psalms that begin with complaint against enemies or, indeed, against God and circumstances, have a way of ending in an exuberance of hope and gratitude.

These ancient poets were not a cautious lot. There is very little in their speech of "Now, on the other hand," or "Of course, I must qualify that statement." We are inclined in our imaginings to picture the writers as men with flowing beards, dignity, and measured stride; we would be closer to the mark if we remembered King David dancing ridiculously in front of the Ark of the Covenant as his aids carried the symbol of God's presence to its home in the Holy City. Some might want to challenge me at this point. The example I have just given is exuberant by nature, so of course people might dance at such a unique time of gladness. But, they might add, the every-week experience of worship, with its established rituals, is another matter. Not as the psalmists saw it. They were writing for the daily reader and for the frequent worshiper, not just for those occasions when faith is stimulated by extraordinary excitements. The note of exuberance is so common in the psalms, so ever-present, even in times of distress, that we must acknowledge that this mood of exuberance is the essence of these ancient Hebrew poets and of the faith that inspired them.

"O sing to the LORD a new song," the psalmist cries; "sing to the LORD, all the earth" (Psalm 96:1). We moderns and postmoderns, committed as we are to the idea that whatever is most recent is best, are likely to think that the psalmist's call for "a new song" is a quest for novelty. I'm sure it's far more than that. His thinking, rather, is akin to the eighteenth-century hymnist and preacher Charles Wesley when he cried, "O for a thousand tongues to sing / my great Redeemer's praise...!" Wesley wrote those words on the first anniversary of his transforming religious experience. Recalling all the wonders of God's work in his life, Wesley found one tongue, yes even a choir, inadequate. Such is the mood of the psalmist. All of his vocabulary seems stunted and insufficient for the wonder he feels, so he yearns for a new way to declare the glory of God. He wants much more than new words, a fresh melody, or a different set of musical instruments; the poet wants a newness within his own person. You've known the frustration, I'm sure, in the experiences of human friendship and love, of saying to someone,

"I just wish I could find the words to tell you what you mean to me" or "what our friendship means to me." So it is that the psalmist wants "a new song." And his exuberance is such that he calls on everyone else to join his choir: "all the earth," "all the peoples."

But our wonderful spiritual ancestor doesn't say, as we might, "I can't find words to express what I feel." He would see this, I think, as an unholy cop-out. So he launches into rolling phrases of praise, making us the richer for it. In a sense, there is nothing new or remarkable about what follows. In the latter portion of the psalm, he pleads for nature to help him express these feelings that strain him almost to the limit. "Let the heavens be glad," "the earth rejoice." He not only wants the sea to "roar," but also wants for "all that fills" the sea to join in. So, too, with the field: He wants it to "exult, and everything in it. / Then shall all the trees of the forest sing for joy / before the LORD" (Psalm 96:11-13).

And what is the reason for such reckless language? In this instance, it isn't what we might expect. So many of our songs of praise, whether in human or divine friendship, seem to come from the benefits the friendship has brought us. The psalmist has a benefit in mind, but in a sense an unlikely one. He rejoices because the Lord "is coming, / for he is coming to judge the earth. / He will judge the world with righteousness, / and the peoples with his truth" (Psalm 96:13). The writer has seen too much inequity in the affairs of earth. He longs for things to be right; that is, for *right*eousness to reign. He wants the judgments of the universe to operate from a base of truth.

The anonymous poet who gave us Psalm 98 operates with the same mood of exuberance, and eventually with the same reason. He or she wants the earth to "make a joyful noise to the LORD," to "break forth into joyous song and sing praises." In his overflow of enthusiasm he calls for an orchestra, or at least a small combo—lyre, trumpets, and horn—to make this "joyful noise." Again, the writer enlists nature. I've seen floodwaters, and they frighten me; he asks the floods to "clap their hands" (Psalm 98:8). There is a national quality in this psalm, however, which is only implied in Psalm 96. This writer is rejoicing in God's "steadfast love and faithfulness / to the house of Israel." God has "revealed his vindication in the sight of the nations" (Psalm 98:2-3). We have no sure indication as to when the poet wrote these words, but they sound as if they came after Israel had won a battle over an oppressing enemy. As the poet sees it, not only has justice come, but it has come from God. He is not subdued when he talks about it. He sings with exuberance.

But for the psalmists, exuberance was not a matter of particular themes, it was a way of life. The moon and the stars evoke the poet's enthusiasm (Psalms 8:3-4; 19:1-6), and so does a violent storm—perhaps even an earthquake (Psalm 18:7-15). I've had some wonderful history teachers in my day, but never one with more enthusiasm for the nation's story than Israel's poets (Psalms 105, 106, 126). The psalmist is excited by the prospect of going to the temple (Psalm 122), and all but overwhelmed by God's vast knowledge (Psalm 139). And when he ponders God's mercy (we would call it grace) in forgiving sin, he reaches for the widest imaginable measure: "as far as the east is from the west, / so far he removes our transgressions from us" (Psalm 103:12). The psalms contain a good bit of complaint, some frantic occasions of doubt and fear, and impassioned cries for help; but in total, they are a veritable extravaganza of praise. Even the psalms that begin in complaint or in fierce supplication have a way of transitioning into cascading gladness.

What makes the psalmists this way? Some would probably explain their exuberance by ethnic and geographical factors. Some people, they would argue, are simply more emotional than others; maybe the psalms would have a different quality if the writers had lived by the Baltic Sea instead of the Mediterranean.

I think this is a point to be reckoned with. Peoples of different areas are often different in the style and extent of their expressions of emotion. We expect the Scandinavian countries to produce heavy, somber movies, and the Russians to give us dark, brooding novels, whereas Spain makes us think of castanets. But of course that isn't explanation enough. Some of us, without a doubt, are more emotional, at least on the surface. Some of us laugh more easily and cry more easily than others. Nevertheless, when I read the sports section of the newspaper, I find that the fans in Philadelphia are altogether as passionate as the fans in Houston, and soccer fans get as emotionally involved in Belgium as in Chile. God (or nature, if you prefer) didn't distribute tear ducts and funny bones selectively. We vary from person to person, but the potential of expression is in us all, and it's generally only a matter of finding what triggers our reaction.

But am I asking too much of this divine-human friendship? Indeed, does my analogy itself fail me? As I said earlier, our human friendships are much more than occasions of dancing and laughter. Some of you would even contend—and with reason—that some of the best moments in friendship are quiet moments. A minister once made the point to me as we ate in a restaurant. He pointed out a couple talking vigorously and said they were dating, while a couple eating almost in silence he identified as married many years; "They don't need to talk," he said. "They're comfortable enough that they can be silent together." True enough, perhaps, and yet one thinks of Tevye, the beleaguered hero of the musical *Fiddler on the Roof,* urging his wife to say that she loved him. He wasn't satisfied by the recital of her daily services of love, he wanted a verbal declaration. The greeting-card business is sustained in a substantial measure, I venture, by friends and family members who are grateful for the stated occasions of life when they can express through a card an exuberance that they otherwise leave silent. I venture further that a vast number of our relationships would be more vital and more fulfilling if we gave them more opportunities for exuberance.

Israel built into its calendar occasions for exuberance. There were not only the annual feast days—all but one of which were celebratory—but every week there was the Sabbath. And the Sabbath was something to be celebrated. It was commanded, yes, but commanded to be sure its rest and restoration were not missed.

Exuberance can't be programmed or scheduled, but a schedule can provide a setting in which exuberance is more easily born or nurtured. That's part of the philosophy of holidays and anniversaries and birthday parties. And it is the very essence of religious ritual. We easily decry "empty ritual"; the Old Testament prophets did so with vigor. But if the ritual is empty, that's our fault. Rituals provide the magnificent setting in which the jewel of holy exuberance can shine.

Faith makes for this exuberance. We can dare to invest ourselves in a relationship, including both the human and divine varieties, because we trust the integrity of the other party. Sometimes, indeed, we trust so deeply in the other party's integrity that we count on them to pick up the slack of our own failures; surely this is the case in our divine friendship. Without such faith and trust, exuberance would be very tentative—and obviously, "tentative exuberance" is an oxymoron.

The secret of exuberance is involvement. If we are to enjoy exuberance, we have to engage ourselves. The more nearly complete the engagement, the greater the level of fulfillment and of exuberance.

And here's the rub for most of us religious folk. We engage in too much of our religion at a safe distance. The saints are those persons—*ordinary* persons—who dare to involve themselves with God unreservedly. They perceive that God has gambled eternal love on them, so they in turn gamble wildly on God. Faith says that this is a safe gamble, because we can count on the character of God. But every saint has had times on the holy journey when he or she wondered if the gamble was badly chosen. Since our vision is limited, we don't always see all that God is about, and we think postponement is indifference or even rejection.

When that's the case, our exuberance can seem not only misdirected, but downright ridiculous. And that's why one needs faith to exercise exuberance. Pity the poor soul who, sometimes because of being disappointed in a friendship or perhaps simply because of a style of upbringing, is afraid to enter into the exuberance of friendship. I trusted once, they say, and all it brought me was disappointment, so I'll never trust again, and thus I'll never be hurt again. But such persons miss the larger fact: By their never trusting again, they never experience the supreme wonders of friendship, including its exuberance.

The ancient psalmists had their times of doubt and disappointment, but they seemed never to lose their willingness to invest themselves in the exuberance of divine friendship. They had tasted of the Lord's goodness, so they wanted more of the wonder they had found. The best of human friendship has its seasons of exuberance. Multiply this experience as far as you can imagine and you see the possibilities of our walk with God. Any day, any hour, any place, we may be at a place where exuberance will sweep us off our feet. If you feel it coming, don't grab hold of some safe hitching post. Let yourself go! There are exuberant possibilities in this friendship beyond our imagining.

Chapter Seven

Secrets of Friendship:
SPECIFICITY

Scripture Reading: Psalms 136 and 150

I suspect that friendships die more often of inattention than of misunderstanding or disagreement. And yes, that which we often call misunderstanding would not have occurred were it not for some earlier instance of inattention. When we have not been properly attentive to another, we prepare the way for misunderstanding. Understanding is built on communication, and obviously enough, when we aren't paying attention to one another communication lapses and misunderstanding naturally takes place.

Of course often the issues within a friendship never reach the point of misunderstanding; it's simply that people grow apart. I expect that all of us can recall some friendship that was once rather cherished, or that at the least seemed to hold promise, but that somehow simply ceased to exist; and recalling it, we can't really explain why it came to an end. We remember no altercation and no real reason why the friendship should not have continued. In the language of theology, there was no sin of commission that broke the friendship, but sins of omission: The friendship died for lack of attention.

Quite clearly, this happens in the divine-human friendship, too. The secret of preventing such a lapse is, of course, to pay attention to the friendship. And in the matter of prayer, this means to fill the language of friendship with *specifics*. I know of very few ways to show that a friendship matters other than to give it the attention that shows itself in being specific. A lazy relationship will be taken over by generalities. A great relationship is marked by the specific. You've been told that the good is the enemy of the best and that the pretty is the enemy of the beautiful. Let me add that the general is the enemy of the specific. The general has its place, of course; but in the most important matters of life, remember the importance of the specific.

We use the general because we're lazy. This is the bane of so many of our discussions of matters both great and small. "*Everyone* knows," we say; or "You *always*," or "People *never*." The moment such a generality comes into speech, quality diminishes, and communication suffers.

One of the grand secrets of prayer, as the psalmists demonstrated it, is the secret of specificity. The psalmists were never lazy in their prayers. They rarely if ever prayed in generalities. We don't hear them saying, "Thanks for everything," or "Bless everybody," or "Forgive my sins." They got down to the proverbial nitty-gritty. They had a passion for listing names, recalling particular events, identifying places. No casual generalities in this friendship!

Let me begin with the remarkable way the writers of the psalms used the first person singular. We tend in our prayers toward the editorial "we," as if a committee were at prayer. Not with the psalmists. Consider that most beloved psalm: "The LORD is *my* shepherd, *I* shall not want. / He makes *me* lie down in green pastures; / he leads *me* beside still waters; / he restores *my* soul" (Psalm 23:1-3, emphasis added). In the New Revised Standard Version, the first person singular appears eighteen times in the six verses of this brief, beautiful psalm.

At first thought, this can seem fearfully self-centered, and of course it can degenerate into that. But it is also honestly and forcefully specific. The psalmist is making his personal testimony. He isn't insisting that God is your shepherd, though hundreds of millions have since declared it so in repeating Psalm 23. But the psalmist has no right to say it for you or for me. He begins with his own experience, and speaks for the only one for whom ultimately he has a right to speak—himself. Sometimes in wanting to be generous and broadminded we actually become presumptuous. We say, "We all believe in the same God," thus embracing some other person in a position they may not want to assume. They may not want to be included with the same God in whom we believe; they may well have positions and convictions of their own, some of which don't fit with "our God."

The psalms are jam-packed with the first person singular. I, my, and me appear repeatedly. Thomas Cahill says that the psalms "are filled with *I*'s: the I of repentance, the *I* of anger and vengeance, the *I* of self-pity and self-doubt, the *I* of despair, the *I* of delight, the *I* of ecstasy" (Thomas Cahill, *The Gifts of the Jews: How a Tribe of Desert Nomads Changed the Way Everyone Thinks and Feels* [New York: Doubleday/ Nan A. Talese, 1998], 199). In the same fashion, the Hebrew poets speak vigorously and insistently of "*You*," in reference to God—or "*Thou*," in some older translations. Dean John B. Coburn said wisely that prayer should begin, "O God, *you*." Because it is only after we have said "God, you," and not "God, he," that we have entered into personal conversation. I become very uneasy with public prayers that begin by addressing God—"Almighty God, we bow before you"—and then shortly indicate that God is not really the other party in the conversation, because the prayer continues, "We pray that God will do thus-and-so." God has somehow gone from being the one addressed to a party referred to in the third person. I sense, in such prayers, that the prayer is really addressed to the congregation or the gathering, rather than to God. So, too, when references are made to Jesus Christ or the Holy Spirit. If the prayer is in truth addressed to God, then a reference to Christ is one to "your Son, our Lord Jesus Christ," and the Holy Spirit is "your Spirit." The conversation is specific; God is the second person in the conversation, not a third person to whom we refer as if we were talking with someone else. The psalmists had this sense of an "I-Thou" conversation—a specific person was talking with a specific Person.

This quality of specificity marks the psalms. As I said earlier, the writers seem to delight in naming names, identifying places, and recalling particular times and events. See in Psalm 108 how the poet recalls God's faithfulness in days past. He doesn't simply thank God for victory over Israel's enemies; he identifies places where victories happened, Israel's particular participants (Gilead, Manasseh, Ephraim, Judah), and the nations Israel has defeated (Moab, Edom, Philistia) (Psalm 108:7-9). When the psalmist repents, he isn't content to make a blanket request for forgiveness. Rather, he uses three different words for sin and three specific words for the kind of action he wants taken to his sins ("Blot out my transgressions. / Wash me thoroughly from my iniquity, / and cleanse me from my sin") (Psalm 51:1-2).

I suspect this dedication to the specific might become tedious to someone whose enthusiasm is not as great as the psalmist's. Psalm 136 was almost surely sung and/or recited antiphonally, with a leader calling out the theme line and the congregation or choir singing the response, through twenty-six verses. The theme lines are specific, whether speaking of the qualities of God, of nature, or of Israel's history. It isn't the sort of song that was written for people in a hurry. But neither is it simply a series of repetitions, except for the choral response. Indeed, that's the sense of the specific. One doesn't thoughtlessly repeat; one carefully finds a new way to carry the theme. We don't "sing that verse" or that line again; we find that each line has an emphasis of its own. That is, it is *specific*. It isn't made for lazy worshipers.

So, too, with the grand climax to the psalms, Psalm 150.

Eventually the writer will conclude, "Let everything that breathes praise the LORD" (Psalm 150:6), but not before calling individually for a response from trumpet, lute, harp, tambourine, dance, strings, pipe, and "loud clashing cymbals" (Psalm 150:3-5). The poet reminds me of a recent evening at the Philharmonic. When the orchestra completed a Saint-Saens piece, we applauded, then came to our feet and continued applauding; and the conductor, like the psalmist, signaled to specific sections to stand—the organist and pianists, the percussionists, several sections of brass, then of strings, until at last the whole orchestra was standing. I said to myself, "The psalmist would like that!"

Specificity saves us from lazy praying. The psalmists won't allow us simply to thank God generally for our blessings; we must, in the language of an old prayer-meeting hymn, "name them one by one." I read recently of a bridal shower where the bride-to-be passed out a stack of envelopes to the guests, asking them to write their name and address on an envelope, so that after the shower the bride could enclose a preprinted thank-you note and mail it to the guest in the envelope the guest had herself addressed! I drew back in unbelief at such an astonishing absence of true gratitude, then pondered how often our expressions of thanks to God are similarly mechanical and lacking in any real heart involvement.

Our thanks to God ought to be wonderfully specific. It isn't enough to thank God for a beautiful day; take the time to note some of the particulars. On occasions, when I'm alone in a hotel room while on a speaking engagement, I will thank God for the favors of the room: the large bed, so different from the beds I knew growing up; the remote for the television set, a convenience I now take for granted but that is a special favor when watching the news at the end of the day from the bed—the many comforts of even an average hotel room that I could not have imagined in the earlier days of my traveling; the soft-drink machine just down the hall, the bottled water in my room, the desk that promises me efficiency when I work, the free newspaper, the large chair or sofa—matters on every side that make life more comfortable, and for which I want to give thanks to God.

I try to follow the same rule of specificity in my petitions. I remember my childhood prayers, when I finished listing family members and playmates with an all-inclusive, "And Lord, bless the whole world, and all the people in it." My intentions were good, and certainly the spirit of inclusiveness was right, but there wasn't much earnest thought in the generality I employed. So I have learned to speak names to God, and as I do, more names come to me. When I was a pastor, I tried when serving Communion to speak to God the names of each person as I offered them the bread and the cup. If it was someone I didn't know, I asked God to touch the person with the knowledge that, even though a stranger to me, they were cared for.

In this matter of petitioning God by specific names, I confess a simple faith, but one that is significant enough to me that I dare to recommend it to you. As I go about each day, numbers of persons come to mind. Some names appear logically—I see the person on the street, or hear from them by letter or e-mail. But some seem to come out of the proverbial blue. I take each such name as a gift from the Holy Spirit, and ask God's blessing on the person. If I know something of the person's circumstances, I speak to God from the particulars of my knowledge; otherwise, I simply recite the name prayerfully. When a person comes to mind unbidden, whether in the middle of the night or while driving or walking or listening to a lecture, I take the name as a divine responsibility. I reason that perhaps it is the Spirit of God that has brought this person to mind, and that by my prayer I may help bring God's will to pass in that person's life. It's a win-win situation. If I am right in thinking that God has prompted my attention to this person's need, I am working with God in bringing God's purposes into being; if the person has come to my mind for no explainable reason, and God has nothing to do with their occurring to me, I am still doing that person good by speaking their name in prayer. And in doing so, I am also drawing closer to that person and closer, indeed, to God.

I seek the same specificity when I confess sin to God. I don't want to be guilty of easy repentance, so that I treat divine grace casually. When Heinrich Heine, the nineteenth-century German poet and essayist, lay dying, his last words were, "God will forgive me; that's his business." Heine was a pretty fair student of religion, so he knew what he was saying, and in a sense, he was making a true and rather profound theological statement. But there's also a casualness about it that probably reflects the thinking of a great many people. I fear many of us confess sin as if God is only performing one of the divine functions when forgiveness is extended.

The psalmists knew better, and prayed accordingly. They didn't abuse grace by lazy generalities; they thought enough of God to *think*, to be specific. Oswald Chambers, a saint of another more recent time, said it perfectly. In the presence of God, Chambers said, he did not see himself as "a sinner in an indefinite sense; I realize the concentration of sin in a particular feature of my life" (Oswald Chambers, *My Utmost for His Highest* [Uhrichsville, Ohio: Barbour and Company, 1993], 185). This does not mean wallowing in our sins; to do so can be a kind of perverted self-centeredness, as if our sins were more notable than average and our self-abasement more complete. But our repentance should go beyond superficial thinking, so we consider why we have sinned, and what it is in us that inclines toward particular failings. With such realization we equip ourselves to walk more uprightly in the future, and to guard against carelessly falling into the same destructive patterns.

We confess our sins, not with innocuous generality, but with specific insight and sorrow. What is it I have done against the majesty of God? How have I abused the goodness God has invested in me through the kindness of so many people? When have I been thoughtless in my relationships this day? It is only as I deal specifically with where I have sinned that I recognize my need of a Savior and of a better way of living. I can never know the wondrous specifics of God's grace except as I face up to the specific facts of my sins that make grace both necessary and amazing.

So it is that the psalmists were not content to stay with generalities when they prayed. They might begin there, but they moved quickly into the ground of real names, real places, real events, the precise and demanding facts of daily life. I don't recognize all the names from their geography or their history, but I pray better because they didn't forget them. Because when we become specific in our prayers, we enter the heart of our dear Friend who numbers the hairs of our head and who sees the sparrow's fall. To engage in friendship with such a God is to avoid casual generalities and to name specific persons, specific needs, specific sins, and specific wonders.

Chapter Eight

Secrets of Friendship:
WONDER AND WITNESS

Scripture Reading: Psalms 23 and 27

You may accept *wonder* as a term appropriate to describing friendship with God, but question how I can apply it to human friendship. There's no problem, really. Most of us come to look upon our best friends with a quality of wonder, though we may not think of using that term. I'm quite realistic about people; reading the Bible has made me so, because the Bible is a wonderfully candid book, never tilting the score in favor of its heroes and heroines. I see my friends for what they are. I generally know their faults as well as their virtues.

But friendship makes me treat both faults and virtues with this quality that I call *wonder*. I think of my friend of longest standing, whom I met in the fifth grade and then came to see as a lifetime friend beginning in our junior year in high school. He was an erratic human being and a high-maintenance friend. But he was always bigger than life to me. When I described him to those who never knew him, or who knew him only casually, I marshaled superlatives with abandon. As for his faults, all his fleas were simply gazelles that had gone wrong. Faults that in others offended me were somehow endearing in Bill. Flaws of character in other people were what made Bill a character. On the whole, I see all my closest friends that way. After all, humans are a remarkable creation, and when you know some human well enough to call him or her a friend, the remarkableness overshadows all else, so that you see the person with wonder.

With that wonder comes the act of witness. I remember the day my high-school debate coach—my hero and mentor—took me aside to counsel me quietly. "Ellie, you'd do well to cut back on your association with Bill. The teachers consider him irresponsible and a troublemaker. Your friendship with him is hurting your reputation." As much as I cherished my teacher's approval, I disregarded his advice. I was sure that if he knew Bill as I did, he would see Bill's virtues. So I insisted on being a witness on Bill's behalf; in this instance, by continuing publicly as his friend when to do so brought my own standing in question. In time, I played a part in Bill's becoming a Christian. Our friendship continued over many decades and a conglomerate of living, until the day of his death; and because I believe, as we say in the Apostles' Creed, in "the communion of saints," I feel close to him still.

The psalmists would understand what I'm saying. They were persons passionate in both human and divine friendship. "A friend loves at all times," the writer of Proverbs insisted (Proverbs 17:17). "All times" is a lot to ask of anyone. I'm usually cautious about such all-encompassing language. But I know why the ancient writer made such a broad declaration; he had experienced friendship at its ultimate, and he needed extravagant language to describe it. The psalmists approached their friendship with God with just such awe and wonder, and often turned their wonder into insistent witness.

The sense of wonder is always there for the psalmist. He may complain about his life and even about the way he thinks God is treating him or neglecting him, yet the sense of wonder is never lost. I know of no literature that so recklessly brings together the immanence of God and the transcendence of God. The psalmist feels God is so approachable that he dares to raise questions about God's very character; then, suddenly, God is so eternal that the poet struggles for words to express his awe.

There's a certain audacity in so many of the psalms, as the writers lay claim to the whole universe in the name of their God. "The earth is the LORD's and all that is in it, / the world, and those who live in it" (Psalm 24:1). If the writer had been an Egyptian, a Babylonian, or a Persian at certain times in their histories, such language would have been defensible, even if hard to prove. But the Hebrew psalmists were announcing the glory of the Lord God from a small stage. Their country was a little one, and except for a brief period in the days of David and Solomon, they were never really a national power to be reckoned with. If the wonder of God was reflected in the power and influence of the people claiming God's name, the case was weak. But this kind of logic didn't faze the Hebrew poets. They insisted with magnificent confidence that the whole earth belonged to their God. So what if their own little piece of real estate was insignificant among the kingdoms of the world! God was God, and the psalmists understood that it was by God's permission that other nations were allowed to stake out their claims.

You'll find the same mood in Psalm 66. Again the writer sweeps his arms around the whole world in the name of God. "Make a joyful noise to God, all the earth; / sing the glory of his name; / give to him glorious praise. / Say to God, 'How awesome are your deeds!' / . . . All the earth worships you; / they sing praises to you, / sing praises to your name" (Psalm 66:1-4). If you had interrupted this poet by asking, "Can you prove that 'all the earth' worships God?" he would probably have answered, "If they don't, they should!" The writers of the psalms are fully satisfied that there is no one to be compared to the Lord God. They may have their times when they question and complain, but when the vote comes in, there is no negative. The God of Israel is *great, and greatly to be praised.* Charles Wesley concluded one of his loveliest hymns with the line, "Lost in wonder, love, and praise." The psalmists would have said amen to that. Or more likely, they would have said to Wesley, "You got the idea from us."

It isn't far from the place of wonder to the place of witness. If we believe deeply in someone, we can hardly refrain from testifying to the beauty we find in him or her. Without a doubt, the favorite psalm is Psalm 23. You don't need a survey to prove it. Most pastors will tell you that if at the time of bereavement they ask the family what scriptures should be read, one choice is almost always Psalm 23. And this is a psalm of witness. The writer, David, tells us, "The LORD is my shepherd, I shall not want. / He makes me lie down in green pastures; / he leads me beside still waters; / he restores my soul" (Psalm 23:1-3). He is reporting on the wonder of a remarkable friendship, and in doing so, he recommends his friend. At no point does he say, "And you should know him, too," but his report is so compelling that we want to inquire where we can come to enjoy such a friendship. As a matter of fact, I suspect this psalm has been as effective an introduction to conversion as any portion of the Bible. It doesn't tell the way to God, but it surely recommends that this is Someone I ought to know. I suspect that all of those people in hospital beds, nursing homes, and settings of sorrow and bereavement who have wanted a pastor to recite or read Psalm 23 have been making a step toward God, and they have done so on the witness of an ancient believer who testified from the wonder of his holy experience.

No doubt you've noticed the rather surprising shift that takes place in this psalm about midway. The writer begins by referring to God in the third person: "The LORD . . . he"—and the writer doesn't indicate to whom he is addressing his remarks. Did he speak these words originally to a friend, or to family? Or perhaps in an act of public worship, in the midst of fellow believers? We have no indication, and in a sense, that's especially lovely, because as a result, we can read the words twenty-five or thirty centuries later and feel he's talking to us. But then, in verse 4, the psalmist begins talking *to* God: The third-person "he" becomes the second-person "you." "*You* are with me; / *your* rod and *your* staff—they comfort me" (Psalm 23:4, emphasis added). And David continues in this style through the remainder of the song until slipping into the third-person address again when he asserts, "and I shall dwell in the house of the LORD / my whole life long" (Psalm 23:6). So it is that the psalm slips back and forth between wonder and witness. At times the poet adores God and talks to God, whereas at other times he seems to be telling some audience or individual what he knows and loves about God.

I find this quality in a number of psalms, this casual movement between wonder and witness. Take Psalm 27, which when put to music in its most familiar form seems almost as lovely as Psalm 23, and perhaps even more majestic. Here, too, the writer begins in the third person, with the language of wonder and witness. As the psalm unfolds, we gather that the writer is reporting on a battlefield experience. "Though an army encamp against me, / my heart shall not fear; / though war rise up against me, / yet I will be confident" (Psalm 27:3). From the vantage point of such a perilous experience, he is filled with awe and wonder that his Friend has seen him through, and he wants now to witness to that fact—again, to whoever will hear. He doesn't choose to identify an audience. Because of the nature of the psalm, one can imagine the writer (again, traditionally identified as David) addressing his comrades on the battlefield, perhaps after the siege is complete or perhaps even in the midst of battle. If it was in the midst of battle, this was easily the most moving halftime, locker-room speech of human history.

And as in Psalm 23, the writer slips naturally and unconsciously from a third-person reference to God to a second-person address. In this case, it is within a matter of half a dozen words. Verse 6 concludes, "I will sing and make melody to the LORD," and verse 7 begins, "Hear, O LORD, when I cry aloud." God, the point of reference, becomes God, the object of petition. In verses 8 and 9, David explains to God what is going on in his mind: "'Come,' my heart says, 'seek his face!' / Your face, LORD, do I seek. / Do not hide your face from me."

And after several verses in which the writer appeals to God—the party of the second part, the joy of his friend-ship—he concludes by a testimony:

> I believe that I shall see the goodness of the LORD
>   in the land of the living.
> Wait for the LORD;
>   be strong, and let your heart take courage;
>   wait for the LORD! (Psalm 27:13-14)

When one reads psalms such as the two that I have just referred to, one wonders what was going on. It's as if the writer couldn't decide whether he was at prayer or in a testimony service. He speaks for a moment as if God alone were the audience, then without warning or transition, seems to be telling someone else about God. In a way, these psalms remind me of a church service in the little Methodist church of my childhood. It was called the "Prayer and Praise Service," and it was a service that moved back and forth between testimonies and moments of prayer. On reflection I have concluded that all that happened was, in its own right, prayer. When we speak gratefully of God's goodness, our words constitute the truest form of thanksgiving; we may be speaking to a friend, but our words acknowledge God. The person who tells someone that he or she is confident of God's help in a passing crisis is witnessing to the character of God while at the same time worshiping God. Perhaps some of our best prayers are the words we speak to others concerning our love for our Lord, our earnest trust, our deep grief that we have in some way failed God.

And more than that. When the psalmist shouts, "The

LORD is my light and my salvation; / whom shall I fear?" (Psalm 27:1), I sense that he is addressing more than some opposing general or an invading army. His is a challenge into the very teeth of hell, into all those elements in life that seem irrational, unfair, and nearly hopeless. When all the structures of life are collapsing and everything that was nailed down is coming loose, the person of faith insists on declaring his or her position: God is God, and ultimately God must win. The psalmist wrote, "My soul makes its boast in the LORD; / let the humble hear and be glad" (Psalm 34:2). Here is the essence of wonder that is also witness. The poet boasts in God—that is, gives thanks and praise to God—and his boast becomes a witness to the humble soul, reminding such a one that boasting has at times its sacred place.

We all have those occasions when life is contrary to our perception of rightness, justice, and holy order. Some of these occasions are so petty that afterward we're ashamed to admit that we were upset; others are so shattering that even the insensitive ask how we have survived. But large or small, these adversities try the soul to the limit. At such times, we should take the language of the psalmists as our own. Looking adversity and injustice in the face, as if they were an enemy battalion, we declare our confidence in God. What we say is an act of worship, an expression of wonder at God's incomparable character; but it is also our witness—to people, perhaps, but to hell, too. Name the demons what you will: injustice, incongruity, irrationality. Then announce to these creatures of torment that you believe in the God who is on the side of justice, the congruent, the magnificently rational. Not only is God on the side of such, God is the very source of such. And our wonder becomes witness.

The Benedictine monk Damasus Winzen says that the Hebrew word *hallel* (the base, of course, of the word *hallelujah*) primarily means "to radiate" or "to reflect" (Kathleen Norris, *The Cloister Walk* [New York: Riverhead Books, 1996], 105). When we worship, the experience of awe reflects the glory we are experiencing. At its best, the

71

wonder we feel becomes a witness to a world and a culture that either hasn't experienced such wonder or that is badly in need of a contemporary witness. Sometimes this witness shows itself as in the psalter, through words we speak. At other times, the witness is reflected in countenance and deeds. But one way or another, the wonder and the witness go together. The psalmists found it so, and so have hosts of lesser-known saints, even to this present day.

Chapter Nine

Secrets of Friendship:
GRATITUDE

Scripture Reading: Psalms 92, 107, 118

Gratitude is the lubricant of life in general, and of friendship in particular. I wonder if there is any language that doesn't have some word or expression to convey the feeling of gratitude. I doubt it. Something in us humans insists on expressing thanks; we say thank you not simply because the other person deserves the word but also because we need to say it. This is so much the case that I sometimes think we're about to eliminate "You're welcome" from our lexicon of courtesy. You thank me for some kindness I have done, and I'm likely to reply, "Thank *you!*" It's as if the person receiving the thanks can't let the matter end there; we want the other party to know that we're grateful for their gratitude, or perhaps that we have as much reason to say thank you as they have.

I may be overstating the case when I suggest that something in us humans insists on expressing thanks. Some of our practice is, of course, a learned custom. Some parent or aunt or grandparent taught us that we should use a particular phrase in response to someone's gift or kindness, and they prompted us in this action until we learned when the term should be employed. But whereas the language and rituals of gratitude may be a learned response, the basic quality is, I think, more instinctual. No doubt it can be killed for a person who lives too long with boorishness and rejection, but it is part of our normal human makeup.

And it finds its best expression in friendship. When the somewhat eccentric genius William Blake said, "Gratitude is heaven itself," he was not far from the mark. Gratitude is a right estimate of our relationship to God, to others, and to life itself, because gratitude is the recognition that no one is a solitary achiever, no one has accumulated success or wealth unaided. Every human being is a debtor. We acknowledge this best in the bonds of friendship, where we find it easier to confess someone else's importance in our lives. With that confession comes a peculiar freedom, the lifting of the weight of imagined self-importance. I am what I am rather largely because of the goodness and kindness and helpfulness of others, including some I will never know this side of eternity.

And then there is God. Gratitude is utterly essential in that language of holy friendship that we call prayer. One cannot stand long in the presence of the Eternal without wanting to break into some song of thanksgiving. The ancient poets, those hearty souls of Israel, did it best.

But before I proceed into some selected psalms, let me express a concern regarding prayer as a whole, and prayers of gratitude in particular. People sometimes make gratitude a means to an end, hoping that by thanking someone they will get something still more. This is a monstrous evil. It contradicts the essence of gratitude and violates its definition. Unfortunately, it is now written into several patterns of our lives. The charity to which we have given includes with its thank-you note a form on which we can enter our next gift. A well-meaning parent urges a child to send a thank-you note with the admonition, "If you want Aunt Esther to remember you on your next birthday, you'd better thank her for what she sent." I warmly support the parent's urging a child to send a letter of appreciation, but I regret the incentive used.

I regret even more the religious teaching that sees gratitude as a means of obtaining still more blessings or of influencing God to be favorable—as if God needed encouragement to be gracious. Unfortunately, this kind of teaching is all too common. Such teaching is not only a perversion of the principle of gratitude; it is a misuse of the gift of prayer. I believe that prayer does, indeed, work miracles. A wall motto in my childhood home declared, "Prayer changes things." I believe that, and I don't at all mind your calling me simple for so believing. I believe that prayer changes not only the one who prays, but under the best circumstances it also changes the situation for which one prays. I don't think this is a matter of magic; I think it involves some divine laws, most of which we understand very poorly, but more particularly it involves God's readiness to cooperate with us in making this world what God wants it to be.

But I don't think there are any rules of prayer or any practices that guarantee divine intervention. When I hear of some teaching that recommends the recitation of key phrases or the use of prescribed rituals as a means of getting more results in prayer, I feel that faith and the Scriptures are being treated obscenely. God is not a tyrant to be bought off or a robot to be manipulated. And although, as I said a moment ago, I think certain divine laws are at work in the world of prayer, I believe that God, by definition, is above all such laws.

Particularly, I insist that prayer should be the language of friendship, and any friendship that is maintained or used for what someone can get out of it is a friendship that is prostituted. We pray because we want to commune with our best and surest Friend. We know that this Friend has the power to respond to our prayers in ways quite beyond our calculating, and I am confident enough in the friendship to ask God's help. But the help is incidental to the friendship. If the help—

that is, the answers to prayer—becomes the end of the friend-ship, God has ceased to be our friend and has become a device, a method, a holy lackey.

All of which is to say that I trust this Friend and our friend-ship enough that if I do not receive the answer I seek, the friendship is unaffected. Indeed, the friendship may even be enhanced, because now I have renewed opportunity to cherish my Friend for the friendship alone (rather than for any benefits the friendship may bring) and to trust my Friend's judgment.

But back to the matter of gratitude. The quality of grat-itude permeates the psalms. I have chosen to look at Psalm 92. This is one of the more than forty psalms whose author is not identified. We don't know if the writer was male or female, young or old, king or commoner, priest or farmer. The writer begins almost prosaically. "It is good to give thanks to the LORD, / to sing praises to your name, O Most High" (Psalm 92:1). I like the word *good*. There's nothing dramatic about it, nothing insistent or overwhelming. But after such a matter-of-fact beginning, the psalmist raises the bar of expectation. This giving of thanks is to be declared "in the morning" and again "by night." And because it's such a right thing to do, the poet calls for musical accompaniment: Bring out the lute, the harp, and the lyre! And why? "For you, O LORD, have made me glad by your work; / at the works of your hands I sing for joy" (Psalm 92:4).

At this point, however, the psalmist becomes quite forth-right. As he (or she) considers God's works, he is openly upset that some people just don't get it.

> Your thoughts are very deep!
> The dullard cannot know,
>   the stupid cannot understand this. (Psalm 92:5-6)

I won't defend the writer's impatience, but I understand it. If you feel great pride in a friend and the friend's accomplishments and character and come upon someone who isn't equally impressed, indeed, who doesn't even seem to care—well, you can't help wondering at the other person's judgment and intelligence. At your best, you might simply feel sorry for such a person, but because it's your friend that is involved, you find yourself slipping into strong and questionable language: Anyone who can't rightly appreciate your friend's worth is a "dullard" and is "stupid." It's difficult not to be defensive when your best friend is involved!

In this particular psalm, the writer is reflecting from a position of strength. His eyes "have seen the downfall" of his enemies, while the "righteous flourish like the palm tree, / and grow like a cedar in Lebanon." The victory is so complete that even in "old age they still produce fruit;" and "they are always green and full of sap" (Psalm 92:12-14).

But what if the circumstances are not so favorable? How then does the poet sing? The answers are everywhere in the psalms. Psalm 118 is a prime example. The poet begins with gratitude that shows itself by calling for anyone in ear's shot to hear: "O give thanks to the LORD, for he is good; / his steadfast love endures forever!" (Psalm 118:1). But soon he lets us know that this song has not come out of an era of blessing. "Out of my distress I called on the LORD" (Psalm 118:5). This, then, is no summer song, celebrating lush fields and fruitful days; this is a song that has been born in days of peril and loss. The writer hints broadly that friends have failed him ("It is better to take refuge in the LORD / than to put confidence in mortals"; v. 8), and that he has been disappointed as well in the customary sources of power ("It is better to take refuge in the LORD / than to put confidence in princes"; v. 9).

But that's not all. His song has come out of one of those perilous seasons of life when even God has become suspect. "The LORD has punished me severely, / but he did not give me over to death" (Psalm 118:18). This experience has in no way diminished his sense of gratitude. Before telling us what a close call he has experienced, he declares, "I shall not die, but I shall live, / and recount the deeds of the LORD" (Psalm 118:17). Sometimes, balanced at the near edge of death, the psalmist gets almost playful in his response to God. "What profit is there in my death, / if I go down to the Pit? / Will the dust praise you? / Will it tell of your faithfulness?" (Psalm 30:9). I love the scene. Lying on the sickbed, having just received a dismal report from his physician, he reminds God of something he feels the Divine may have forgotten: "You have a pretty good thing here in me. I'm one of the persons who thinks well of you and who speaks on your behalf. Just remember, if you allow my life to be cut off, your support team will be seriously weakened. My testimony will be lost when they throw dust on me."

Perhaps the grandest element in this quality of gratitude as friends know it is its reckless and wonderful range. Friends are as likely to recall with gratitude a meal at a fast-food stop as one in a five-star restaurant; they rejoice as gladly in the day they were caught in a drenching rain as the walk in soft sunlight. They are grateful for a friendship that is sturdy through the valley of the shadow of death and exuberant in the gladness of well-earned success. And so it is with the psalmists as they rejoice in God. The horizons of gratitude are boundless. They reach from the present moment to the momentous, from what may well be forgotten tomorrow to that which shapes history; from the embarrassingly personal to the world of international politics. In it all, the psalmists see the hand of God, and are grateful.

The writer of Psalm 107 gives us a series of vignettes. His orchestra is hardly seated before he leads us in a robust declaration: "O give thanks to the LORD, for he is good; / for his steadfast love endures forever" (Psalm 107:1). Then he unfolds his scenarios of God's goodness. First, there are those who wander in "desert wastes," so "hungry and thirsty [that] their soul fainted within them." No matter! "For [God] satisfies the thirsty, / and the hungry he fills with good things" (Psalm 107:4-9). Then there are those who "sat in darkness and in gloom, / prisoners in misery and in irons" (v. 10).

We're ready to sympathize with them, thinking they're in such a state in innocence. But as it happens, they're here because they had "spurned the counsel of the Most High." We can expect, then, that God might let them get their deservings here. Not so, the psalmist reports. When these cry out to the Lord "in their trouble," God saves them from their distress; God "shatters the doors of bronze, / and cuts in two the bars of iron" (Psalm 107:13, 16).

So, too, with those who "because of their iniquities endured affliction" (Psalm 107:17). God isn't pleased with sin, so this promises to be a sad story. But when these—these clearly unworthy ones—cry out to the Lord, he saves them "from their distress; / he sent out his word and healed them" (Psalm 107:19-20). And so the poet continues. God sustains those who go "down to the sea in ships" (v. 23)—a way of life not native to the Israelites; they generally left that world to their neighbors in Tyre and Sidon. At the other extreme, God shows faithfulness in the desert places, turning "a parched land into springs of water," so that "he does not let their cattle decrease" (Psalm 107:35, 38). He concludes this remarkable song, with its series of one-act dramas of God's faithfulness, with the counsel of experience: "Let those who are wise give heed to these things, / and consider the steadfast love of the LORD" (Psalm 107:43). His stories have a wide-ranging series of plots, but one theme runs through them all: gratitude to the Lord God.

Almost surely someone has confided to you after the death of a family member or a friend, "I wish I could have told her just one more time how much she meant to me." This is the true language of friendship. I have heard it at times from people who had reason to regret, because they had been neglectful. But I've heard it, too, from those who visited a friend or family member daily and who expressed gratitude over a lifetime, yet felt now, at death's entry, that not enough gratitude had been spoken.

Those who have known God best sense this frustration—that having said all, still they will not have said enough.

William Cowper, known among scholars as one of the best minor poets of the eighteenth century, and better known among Christians as a cofounder of the *Olney Hymnal,* felt this frustration. Ever since he had found faith in Christ, he wrote, "Redeeming love has been my theme, / And shall be till I die." That isn't enough, however, so Cowper could have despaired. Instead, he wrote:

> Then in a nobler, sweeter song,
>   I'll sing thy power to save,
> When this poor, lisping, stammering tongue
>   Lies silent in the grave.
> ("There Is a Fountain Filled with Blood," ca. 1771)

The psalmists only rarely seemed to grasp the idea of life beyond the grave, so they couldn't find Cowper's solace. I'm grateful to be in Cowper's position, believing I will have eternity to continue my expressions of gratitude. But I don't want the promise of eternity to excuse my possibilities here. I want, with Isaac Watts, to promise, "My days of praise shall ne'er be past, / While life, and thought, and being last." This greatest, most faithful, eternal Friend deserves such unceasing gratitude; through time and eternity.

Not only does God deserve my gratitude, I need desperately to speak it, because something in human nature needs to say *thank you.* When we fail to say it, we are less than what God made us to be. And when we fail to speak it to God, we lose some of the exquisite joy of our eternal friendship.

Chapter Ten

Secrets of Friendship:
REPENTANCE

Scripture Reading: Psalm 51

Someone has said that the two most important words in the English language are "I'm sorry." These words probably also rank high among the words most difficult to say. That figures. Anything so important will of course come with a price, and the price is high when one says, "I'm sorry." These two simple words are a confession of imperfection, and quick as we are to say, "Nobody's perfect," we hate to get specific about it; perhaps we're so quick to declare general human imperfection in the hope that no one will get specific and personal about it. "I'm sorry" is also a declaration of trust; once we've spoken these words to someone, that person has a certain power over us, perhaps even superiority. The words are a gamble, too, because after I've told you I'm sorry, I have to wonder if you will accept my regret and forgive me, or if instead you will choose to exploit my vulnerability.

Erich Segal contributed a sentence to our public memory through his novel *Love Story* and the movie that came from it: "Love means not ever having to say you're sorry." This may be true if we love someone in such a way that we don't care what the other person does, but such a relationship would lack mutuality, since it would call for unfathomed depth in one person while fostering superficiality in the other. Most of us have heard someone say regretfully of a friendship, "I never heard him say he was sorry." Even the most earnest friendship or the most ecstatic marriage needs these two words, because even though one may not have caused hurt intentionally, all of us in our humanness sometimes speak an unfortunate word or commit a thoughtless deed; and though no malice was intended, we still need to say, "I'm sorry"—not because we intended to bring hurt, but because the other person has suffered pain. In friendship, regret goes deep and demands expression.

The loveliest of all friendships, the God-human one, is blessed with the most eloquent expressions of "I'm sorry." I doubt that there is any place in literature where the sorrow of a broken relationship is more passionately declared than in some of the psalms. Scholars identify seven psalms as "Penitential Psalms"—psalms 6, 32, 38, 51, 102, 130, and 143. But I'm impressed that words of repentance break quite naturally into other themes. The psalmists don't seem to need an immediate reminder or a liturgy of penance; their hearts are sensitive enough that even while praying about other matters, they interrupt themselves to repent.

In Psalm 25, in the midst of a prayer for guidance, David suddenly cries, "For your name's sake, O LORD, / pardon my guilt, for it is great" (Psalm 25:11). What made him say such a thing at that moment? And how is it that he senses that his dereliction is "great"? A heart of friendship is open to correction. Now and again the psalmists pray for judgment on their enemies, but sometimes they catch themselves in the process and examine their own souls, lest their cry for divine vengeance get completely out of hand. In Psalm 139, the writer has just asked God to send judgment on his enemies; but without pausing for a breath he continues, "Search me, O God, and know my heart; / test me and know my thoughts. / See if there is any wicked way in me, / and lead me in the way everlasting" (Psalm 139:23-24). The writer thinks he is right, and thinks it deeply enough that he is ready to pray judgment on someone else. And yet, he pauses to confess that he just could be wrong, that there might be some "wicked way" in him, so he urges God to search out his heart. He invites the convicting guilt that will compel him to repent.

It must also be said, however, that if one reads the psalms in their entirety, one finds a great many instances where the psalmists seem to compliment themselves on their goodness. In his little book on the psalms, George S. Gunn said that people "in every age have found it hard and uncongenial to accept the fact that sin is exceedingly serious and that it is in them all in that form" (George S. Gunn, *Singers of Israel* [Nashville: Abingdon Press, 1963], 62). I am sometimes uncomfortable when I hear the psalmist speaking so assuredly of his own merit. Some would reply that I was probably raised on a good deal of self-condemnation. Perhaps, though I doubt that it was excessive. Then, too, it may be that the psalmists were, in the particular instances of self-appraisal, being necessarily defensive. There are times when we ought to speak a good word for ourselves. Indeed, sometimes we attack ourselves with a virulence that would cause us to rise up in wrath if the same words were spoken by another. So let's say a cautiously good word for the psalmists in their readiness to speak well of themselves. I say "cautiously good" because you and I belong to a culture that is so intent on nurturing delicate egos that we're generally more in need of recognizing our sins than of boasting of our virtues. No matter; we ought above all to be honest with God, and in those instances where we have gained ground in the pursuit of righteousness or where this time we have done good where at other times we've done bad, let us be honest in accepting the goodness, and be thankful.

But back to the burden of this chapter. Friendship needs repentance. When things have gone wrong, they need to be made right. We all know those instances in both real life and in literature where a friendship has been violated in one way or another, and the offending party has chosen not to deal with the matter. In some cases, this negligence has come because the offending party wasn't sensitive enough to recognize the lapse. Years go by, and the matter is not forgotten. One day when some other issue is at stake, the offended party brings up the old hurt: "You never made it right. You didn't acknowledge your wrong at the time, and you've never dealt with it." And the two parties discover that what was once perhaps a relatively minor matter has now become a devastating rupture. We need the gift of repentance.

But that's only part of the issue in this matter of repentance. Repentance is crucial not only for our relationship with another; it is an equally crucial quality in a person's relationship with his or her own soul. Dean W. R. Inge, a theologian who was also a pungent observer of the human scene, once said, "Prayer gives a [person] the opportunity of getting to know a gentleman he hardly ever meets. I do not mean his maker, but himself." Repentance is key to the knowing of ourselves. We'll never get very deep into self-knowing without feeling the need to repent, to be sorry—before God, before those closest to us, perhaps even to the human race as a whole.

If the process of repentance is worthy of the name, we engage in the deepest kind of soul-searching, and in the process we rid ourselves of a great deal of garbage. Environmental experts tell us that our nation's metropolitan areas are in danger of being overrun by rubbish. What is physically true of our cities is still more painfully and eternally true of our souls. Unconfessed sin, whatever its form—bitter memories, resentments, thoughtless words, moral and ethical betrayals—will eventually stifle the soul unless it is dealt with. The human soul can endure only so much garbage; repentance consumes it in a merciful conflagration.

Tradition says that King David wrote Psalm 51 after the prophet Nathan confronted him concerning his sin with

Bathsheba. The "feel" of the psalm surely supports that idea. When we read David's story in several books of the Old Testament, we understand why he is described as someone after God's own heart. Very clearly, David was a person who passionately desired God. He was far from a perfect human being. But whatever his failures, he longed for God. In Psalm 51 we see the exquisite agony of a friendship in peril. It seems utterly clear that its author can endure any loss in his life if only this friendship can be saved.

He stakes his claim within the opening sentence: His appeal for God's forgiveness rests on God's "steadfast love," the magnificent Hebrew word *hesed*—a word quite beyond full definition, but along with grace surely the ultimate expression of God's readiness to enter into friendship with us humans. David counts on this quality in God as his assurance that God will hear his prayer and will accept his repentance.

His distress over his sin is so great that he searches for words. He uses three different words—transgression, iniquity, and sin, in our English translation—to identify his wrongdoing, and calls upon three actions from God to deal with the enormity of what he has done—blot out, wash, cleanse. What he has done is in his eyes so monstrous that it is "ever before me." Look right, look left, it is there; whatever the scenery, whatever the distractions, whatever the engagements of life, always and always and always one thing is there, inescapable: the sin he has done, the deed and its accompanying state of mind that now threaten his dearest possession, his eternal friendship.

In most instances when we have violated a friendship, we tend to look for a justification. We're sometimes altogether too ready to spread the blame around. Not so with the psalmist. "Against you, you alone, have I sinned, / and done what is evil in your sight, / so that you are justified in your sentence / and blameless when you pass judgment" (Psalm 51:4). If this psalm was written after David's sin with Bathsheba and Uriah, it seems to us that he has sinned against his family, his nation, and quite surely against

Bathsheba and Uriah. But David has a clear sense of sin; sin is an act against God because sin is so surely a God issue. And David knows that what he has done will therefore destroy his divine friendship unless somehow he can clear the matter with the One against whom ultimately his evil has been done.

My whole person joins David when he prays, "Do not cast me away from your presence, / and do not take your holy spirit from me" (Psalm 51:11). As I said earlier in this book, I am not so noble as to invite a dark night of the soul in order to have a deeper walk with God. I cannot bear the prospect of God's Spirit departing from me. Whatever else you ask, O God, allow me the presence of your Spirit. I understand the pathos of David's cry.

Several qualities are no doubt missing from a good deal of religious experience as it is commonly known in our day, but perhaps nothing is more serious than our failure to see the need for repentance. I think this is partly because we don't understand the nature of sin. If, as some contemporaries say, other generations were guilt obsessed, our generation is expert in avoiding the sense of guilt. This is because we have so limited a theology of sin. We define sin by tabloid headlines, which give most of us a degree of comfort, since our sins are only occasionally so dramatic. We don't realize that sin, even as we experience it in its most pedestrian forms, is a violation of the very nature of our universe, a universe whose original core is utterly right because it is of God. We have a further handicap in that our theology of God is inadequate. Popular theology has made God so cozy and so accessible that we can't understand why the Eternal One should be troubled by our erratic ways.

But above all, we fail at repentance because our friendship with God has so little passion. The Scriptures say that we should love the Lord our God with all our heart, soul, mind, and strength. That's the language of passion, the language we generally reserve for moments of compelling romance or consuming friendship. It is only when God becomes such a friend—yes, and far more, because the element of eternity enters into this friendship—that we are struck with terror at the thought of losing this friendship. It is in such a mood that godly repentance is born.

I find no formula for repentance in the psalms. The very idea seems almost obscene. George Croly, the nineteenth-century poet, pleaded with God for "one holy passion, filling all my frame," and with the goal that his heart might be "an altar" and God's love "the flame" ("Spirit of God, Descend upon My Heart," *The United Methodist Hymnal* [Nashville: The United Methodist Publishing House, 1989], 500). This longing for the divine friendship is not a set of rules or a packaged prescription. Psalm 51 is nothing so much as a devastated penitent, someone who is so distraught by what he has done that he cries out, "I was born guilty, / a sinner when my mother conceived me" (v. 5). At this moment it seems to him that the evil within him has been with him forever, from before conscious memory, so that now all he wants is that God should restore to him the joy of his salvation.

I am impressed that the psalmist never tells us whether forgiveness has been given. The Catholic priest assures the penitent that he or she is forgiven; in many of our Protestant services of Holy Communion, the confession of sins is followed by the declaration, "In the name of Jesus Christ, you are forgiven." There is no such statement in Psalm 51. But I feel David's sense of forgiveness when he writes:

The sacrifice acceptable to God is a broken spirit;
a broken and contrite heart, O God, you will not despise.
(Psalm 51:17)

He has brought to God all that he has to offer, "a broken and contrite heart," and he is satisfied that God will judge it to be enough.

I think I understand this. If one cherishes a friendship ultimately, the need to repent is even greater than the need to be forgiven. Something in the soul says, "I want desperately for our relationship to be restored; but above all, I want you to know how sorry I am that I have violated our friendship. To forgive is yours; to repent is mine."

But if you have followed me carefully through this book, you're probably troubled at an apparent omission in this chapter. In human friendship, both parties have reason at times to repent. Since God does no wrong, however, there seems a serious imbalance in the divine-human friendship. It's a good matter to question, and one that deserves a far longer and more complicated answer than I can give in passing.

But let me offer some modest thoughts. We notice, for one, that when God seemed set on destroying Israel during the journey from Egypt to Canaan, Moses pleaded with God. The writer of Exodus continues, "And the LORD changed his mind about the disaster that he planned to bring on his people" (Exodus 32:14); or as the King James Version puts it, "the LORD repented." Both phrases work, because of course to repent is to change one's mind. Some doctrines would insist that God can't repent since God can't be wrong; therefore the language is simply accommodating itself to our human way of seeing and expressing.

Perhaps. In truth, I'm sure that the nature of God is far too complex to fit neatly into even the most sophisticated doctrinal structure. But let's put it this way: I spoke earlier about the repenting we do—the sorrow we feel—when even unintentionally we hurt someone we cherish. I perceive God feeling such sorrow for our failures, and the pain we suffer as the result of our failures. I dare to imagine God saying, "Perhaps I'm expecting too much of these mortal creatures." I see in God a heart that wants us so much as to go the more-than-halfway that pure friendship readily travels. That's the essence of the cross: that God so loves us as to seek us out, because of the pain God feels for our pain. It seems to me that the quality I'm describing comes pretty close to the inner purity of repentance.

You and I are sinners, no doubt about that. We hardly need a doctrine or a story from Eden to prove it, because our own hearts come hard against the fact dozens of times a day—sometimes in sins committed and sometimes in sins contemplated. But we are also creatures with a God-shaped void, who need the eternal Friendship. Repentance copes with the human fact of sin and reengages us with God. The psalmists knew it well, and in God's goodness they provided us with words that help us keep the eternal Friendship clean, pure, and strong. And God is of such a heart as to meet us far more than halfway.

Chapter Eleven

Secrets of Friendship:
HELPLESSNESS

Scripture Reading: Psalm 18

Let me say it before you do: The title of this chapter doesn't appeal to you. You and I deal in self-sufficiency, in being able to carry our share of the load, and if necessary, not needing anybody. It's probably this quality that especially bothers us about going to the hospital. They dress us in garments that substantially reduce our dignity, make us eat when we're told to, puncture us at the times and to the degree they feel necessary, and in total, make us feel very nearly helpless. We don't like it, and we wouldn't put up with it if we didn't think it necessary to our life and well-being.

So an occasional situation of helplessness is enough—like perhaps once in a lifetime. Why would I want to celebrate such an issue by dedicating an entire chapter to the theme, thus indicating that helplessness is a key element in our eternal friendship? To be honest, I don't like this helplessness theme, either. I may like it even less than some of you do. I'm an irrationally independent sort. I will walk a mile to a pay phone rather than ask a neighbor if I can use their telephone.

When I read that the best way to make friends of some people is by letting them do something for us, I decide I can get along with a smaller base of friendship. Believe me, helplessness doesn't appeal to me.

But I have learned by experience that helplessness is one of the loveliest elements in friendship, both human and divine. I remember driving into New York City a very long time ago. How long ago? Long enough that I was driving a De Soto automobile; not many of you will recognize that mark of timing. My world was collapsing around me. I didn't realize it at the time, but my troubles were almost entirely of my own making. Somehow I found my way through a maze of streets to Fifty-sixth Street and Eighth Avenue, where my friend Bill was waiting. I don't think I knew quite how helpless I was, but my coming to New York was hard evidence. My friend Bill saw me through. I was sometimes obnoxious; helpless people often are, because they easily become defensive. There was little in me to admire. Bill didn't seem to care. On one day of enlightenment I told Bill how grateful I was for his friendship. He brushed aside my thanks. "You'd do the same for me," he said. In the years that followed, our friendship was several times put to the test. The sustaining element, I'm sure, was in our memory of days of helplessness.

Multiply that experience by infinity and you have an idea of the element of helplessness that marks our friendship with God. That factor of friendship pervades the book of Psalms. If there is a particular subject about which those ancient saints were authorities, it is the subject of helplessness, and the friendship with God that sustained them in their days of helplessness.

Among the many psalms that demonstrate—indeed, celebrate—helplessness, I especially like Psalm 18. It is long enough to embrace several elements of this particular experience and the moods that accompany it, and it shows wide command of the language of utter helplessness. The ancient notation at the beginning of the psalm advises us that David addressed these words to the Lord "on the day when the

LORD delivered him from the hand of all his enemies, and from the hand of Saul." Those were, indeed, bitter days in David's life. He had gone from being the darling of his nation to a fugitive in danger of his life. The king whose throne David had saved by his heroism with Goliath was now his maniacal enemy. He was cut off from family and from his closest earthly friend, Jonathan. He had surrounded himself with several hundred fighting men, but they were a motley crew of discontents, the kind of persons who could turn against him with the same ferocity that brought them to him. With King Saul insistently on his trail, David's chances of survival were very small. After all, there must have been many citizens in Israel who would have been glad to betray David in order to win the favor of the king. David's road was a lonely, nearly hopeless one.

David's prayer begins, "I love you, O LORD, my strength" (Psalm 18:1). It's a strange combination, isn't it? "Love" is such a gentle word, and "strength" such a robust one. But this is the essence of the prayer of helplessness. We seek from a base of love, and we solicit power to live. This is a mood born of the nursing infant who clings to the breast in trusting love and draws from it the very strength of life. It is the small boy holding his father's hand on a crowded street: love and strength. It is a child of God, of whatever age, surrounded by the armies of hell, taking hold of with love the indomitable strength of God. Helplessness as a word may not appeal to us, but as an experience, it is universal and lifelong. Perhaps it is even necessary. Without it, we would be incomplete as humans, because we wouldn't know the full dimensions of friendship, either human or divine.

Looking back on his recent faith experience, David can hardly find images enough to describe the way God has worked in his life: rock, fortress, deliverer, shield, horn of my salvation, stronghold. All are powerful words, the language of a fighting man, and dramatic evidence of God's work in his life; and yet, such a rush of words that you feel the writer is struggling to say what he's feeling. This, too, I understand, and so do you, if at some point in your life you have blubbered away to a friend, "I just don't know how to thank you"; or while seeking help you have half-sobbed, half-mumbled a jumble of incoherencies. Any eloquence we feel at a time of helplessness is usually found in the quality of the emotions rather than the structure of words.

But the psalmists were artists, and of course in most instances (perhaps all) they recorded their feelings after the fact. You and I can be grateful for that, because thus they have left for us language to communicate our helplessness to God. The structure of Hebrew poetry, to which I have referred earlier, with its repeated lines, seems especially effective for this mood, as the writer declares his need once, then twice, perhaps three times, but with variations that intensify the expression. David writes:

> The cords of death encompassed me;
>   the torrents of perdition assailed me;
> the cords of She'ol entangled me;
>   the snares of death confronted me.
> In my distress I called upon the LORD;
>   to my God I cried for help. (Psalm 18:4-6)

God's response, as David reports it, is adequate to the need. He reports that "the earth reeled and rocked; / the foundations also of the mountains trembled / and quaked, because [God] was angry" (Psalm 18:7). If you need help and need it badly, it's very comforting when the object of your petition becomes passionate about your cause. When I see myself a victim of injustice, I don't want to be greeted impassively; I want my benefactor to declare indignantly, "They can't treat *you* like that!"

Other generations of saints have found their way to speak their helplessness. That remarkable seventeenth-century poet/pastor, George Herbert, wrote of his "affliction":

> My heart did heave, and there came forth, O God!
> By that I knew that thou wast in the grief,
> To guide and govern it to my relief.

It was in the helpless cry to God that Herbert felt assured that God was with him in his grief. If there hadn't been such a realization, Herbert wrote, "Sure the unruly sigh had broke my heart" (George Herbert, "Affliction (3)," in *The Complete English Poems* [New York: Penguin, 1991], 66). François Mauriac, the distinguished French novelist, playwright, and essayist, won the Nobel Prize for his literary excellence, but when he wrote of his walk with God, he spoke with the helplessness of a little child. He goes to his morning prayers, hardly in need of a watch ("I know the time almost to the minute").

> And what do I do then? Well, I sometimes recite a few Latin prayers I learned by heart in my childhood. . . . And why all this Latin at this particular hour rather than at another? Because, as I emerge from sleep, my mind is too sluggish to invent words to converse with the Father as a son should. And so this son relies on the ancient orisons, installing himself in them as a courtier used to install himself in one of the gala carriages which took him where the king wished, without his needing to think about it. (Francois Mauriac, *The Inner Presence*, translated by Herma Briffault [Indianapolis: Bobbs-Merrill, 1965], 135)

Jesus said that we must come to God as little children. This is the essence of helplessness. I'm fascinated that a person of Mauriac's incisive eloquence often found himself so short of words that he resorted to the familiar Latin of his childhood Catholicism to carry his soul to God.

Of course something in our souls reacts to the idea of such helplessness. What's the value of such helplessness? Is it somehow a boost to the divine ego that we are at times forced to a cowering position? Couldn't prayer be just as effective if we were always able to stride purposefully forward, lord and lady of all we survey?

I'm really quite sure that the divine ego will survive without our brokenness, but I'm equally sure that our egos become quite insufferable unless now and then we are compelled to declare some kind of spiritual bankruptcy. Just as we never learn except as we admit ignorance, there are places in prayer that we cannot experience except from the posture of helplessness. At such times of consummate need we learn things not only about the person extending friendship, but also about our own person. We probably know very little about ourselves until we see what we are like when backed into a corner or at the end of our rope.

The psalmists emerged from their experiences of helplessness as better persons. David prayed in Psalm 25, "[God] leads the humble in what is right, / and teaches the humble his way" (Psalm 25:9). One must be humble to be led, because following is a tacit admission the other person knows something we don't. That's probably why some of us would rather wander in confusion around a city than ask for directions. So, too, if we are to be taught, we have to "humble [our] way." Any of us who have tried to teach have learned how difficult it is to instruct those who already—by their own declaration—know everything.

And it may surprise you, but in the process of helplessness those ancient saints gained self-confidence. We live just now in a culture that seems to think we are best served by never hearing a discouraging word about ourselves. In truth, this produces persons with the character of a cream puff. It is as we face the truth about ourselves and as we deal with life's ordinary and extraordinary struggles that we gain strength.

No wonder, then, that David marks his prayer with exuberant declarations of strength. "By you I can crush a troop," he cries, "and by my God I can leap over a wall" (Psalm 18:29). I think he would not have known his audacious potential if he had not come to its definition by way of helplessness. And again, "He made my feet like the feet of a deer, / and set me secure on the heights. / He trains my hands for war, / so that my arms can bend a bow of bronze" (Psalm 18:33-34). As he views the battlefield, David smiles: "You gave me a wide place for my steps under me, / and my feet did not slip." From such a position of strength, of course he can say, "Your help has made me great" (Psalm 18:35-36). Be certain this is a greatness he could never have found except by way of helplessness. I confess readily that I don't like the feeling of helplessness, but I love the strength that comes by way of such abnegation.

And I love, too, the deliverance this helplessness brings. In another psalm that emphasizes helplessness, Psalm 25, David wrestles with *shame,* that vicious hold that others can put upon us. Notice always the difference between *guilt,* which is largely an internal matter between us and our own souls, and *shame,* which is inflicted from the outside by the judgments and expectations of others. In Psalm 25 David turns to God in helplessness, and in the process is delivered from shame. Helplessness before God makes us wonderfully less vulnerable to the judgment of others. Having contemplated our limitations before the Eternal, we are marvelously independent of the transient, no matter how vigorously the transient flaunts itself.

But perhaps I sense a question that troubles you. There ought to be some equity in friendship, some balance. Admittedly, there's a limit to this factor of friendship when the union is between God and us humans. But isn't there at least an element? Is the weight entirely on God's side? Specifically, it's easy to see that we humans have a posture of helplessness before God, but is there any sense in which God has some feature of helplessness in relationship to us?

At first the question seems ridiculous. After all, by definition God is omnipotent; there is no limitation in God, so how can our human-divine friendship include any expression of helplessness on God's part? In this, God has chosen self-imposed limitations.

The mood throughout Psalm 18 (as well as throughout

Psalm 25, and indeed, through the whole body of Scripture) is a mood of battle. David is in conflict. He believes God is concerned about his conflict, and that in a very real, significant sense the conflict matters as much to God as to him. Why? Because David believes that the enemies he fights are not simply his enemies, or Israel's; they are also the enemies of God.

Now I pause long enough to warn both you and me of the danger inherent in this kind of thinking. Vast harm has been done throughout human history, in every expression of religion, by those who have demonized their enemies and have assumed that God is inevitably on their side. But with that precaution we must also acknowledge that our universe is in a massive struggle between good and evil. If we know anything about God, it is surely that God is good, and is on the side of good. Our business, always, is to be sure that we are on the side of good with God. This assurance requires constant humility and self-examination, since we humans are so quick to baptize our convictions with holy significance.

But—and here is the heart of the matter for our purposes just now—God has chosen to leave in our hands the issues of the daily battle between good and evil. We will deal with this matter more fully in the chapter that follows. But for now, let us ponder that God has placed the welfare of this planet in our control. We believe that ultimately God and goodness will win. But in every given day, the issues of the battle are ours. We complain, in the face of tragedy and sin, "Why doesn't God do something?" If we would listen quietly to the Scriptures and the saints, we would hear God answer, "What do you think I have *you* for? For now, the battle is in your hands."

So it is that our dearest Friend, our God, relinquishes power and waits with divine humility for our help. God chooses to take on an element of helplessness, in this friendship where the evidence of helplessness is so obviously ours. But together, by divine grace, we bring about the purposes of God's eternity.

Chapter Twelve

Secrets of Friendship:
ANGER

Scripture Reading: Psalm 139

We know our friends best when we see how ready they are to go to battle for us. I suspect I learned this truth early, probably in some backyard even before kindergarten, but I remember the proof most sharply from an experience much later in my life. In this struggle, I was not entirely in the right; we rarely are, you know. But I watched with sometimes painful, sometimes happy fascination as my friends divided into three parts: Those who now proved not to be my friends at all, but persons who rather easily turned against me; those who were not strongly for or against me (they simply faded into life's woodwork, in truth); and those who drew vigorously to my side, ready to help in any way possible. They didn't actually go into battle for me, of course; my situation wasn't physical, nor did it call for public declarations. But I knew these people were on my side, and as far as I was concerned, they could as well have taken up arms in my defense, so significant was their support.

I believe in anger, rightly used, and I believe deeply in its

99

importance in friendship. If I am treated unjustly, I want friends who will get angry about it, and who will put their anger to productive ends. Anger—because it is so often misused—has gotten a bad name. But anger is essential to human progress. I doubt that many frontier schools would have been built if it had not been for a few parents who got angry with ignorance, or that political reform would ever have taken place except as citizens have gotten angry with civic corruption. The organization "Mothers Against Drunk Driving" has rightly aimed to get the acronym MADD. I worry about people who can live in the midst of economic injustice, exploitation of children, and perversion of the political system without feeling some old-fashioned righteous indignation. True, anger is a dangerous power, but less dangerous than supine acquiescence to evil.

The psalmists were often angry persons. Some of the most violent language in the Bible is in the book of Psalms. Ironically, sometimes the violent language is only a breath or two away from the language of holy adoration. Many people read the psalms so selectively that they never face this anger, but anyone who reads the book all the way through confronts this anger repeatedly. Some purposely avoid such psalms. Dietrich Bonhoeffer, who entered battle against the evils of Nazism, and who loved the book of Psalms and found it especially comforting in prison in the time before his martyrdom, saw it differently. He said that we shouldn't "pick and choose" in our reading of the psalms, as if we know better than God about what we should pray.

Sometimes these psalms (often identified as "imprecatory psalms") have to do with personal injustice, where the psalmist is the victim. In a psalm attributed to David, a prayer for "deliverance from enemies," the writer insists that his enemies have "hid their net for me; / without cause they dug a pit for my life"; then he challenges God, "And let the net that they hid ensnare them; / let them fall in it—to their ruin" (Psalm 35:7-8). It's a rare soul who can't understand that language! I remember a young man who was being vic-

timized by an unjust supervisor. When I asked how he was
dealing with the problem, he answered, "I'm reading the
psalms a lot these days."

The psalmists wrote in such fashion because they believed
that God is just; and therefore, that God has built justice and
integrity into our very universe. It seemed to them that to
ignore such evil conduct was to become party to it. So
another psalmist pleaded with God to "remember this, O
LORD, how the enemy scoffs, / and an impious people reviles
your name." How have they done so? By their treatment of
the poor: "Do not forget the life of your poor forever. . . . Do
not let the downtrodden be put to shame; / let the poor and
needy praise your name" (Psalm 74:18-21). A God who is
not just, and who doesn't care about the mistreatment of
"the poor and needy" would not be worthy of worship. The
psalmists knew that, and prayed accordingly. As surely as the
prophets preached for holy justice, the psalmists prayed for
it.

In his remarkable little book on the psalms, C. S. Lewis
made a vigorous case for the imprecatory psalms. He insisted
that if we can live with evil in the world and not be upset,
something is wrong with us. "The absence of anger, especially that sort of anger which we call *indignation*, can, in my
opinion, be a most alarming symptom. . . . If the Jews cursed
more bitterly than the Pagans, this was, I think, at least in
part because they took right and wrong more seriously"
(C. S. Lewis, *Reflections on the Psalms* [London: Geoffrey
Bles, 1958], 30).

I admit that sometimes the vigor of the psalmist's anger is
more than I can handle. But I'm not in his shoes, nor am I
"wired up" as he was. The psychic pain threshold of indi-
viduals varies just as much, I'm sure, as does the threshold
for physical pain. All of us respond more passionately when
the incident is closer to home, and even within the same
circle many of us respond with different levels of intensity.
The Hebrews had a high sense of justice; to them it was a
matter not only of equity but of godliness. They cared for the

poor, and they believed God did. They were incensed at the thought of injustice, and they believed not only that God was of the same mind, but that it was God who had given them such a perception of life's rightness and wrongness. So while I may be uneasy with the language the psalmist employs, I will try to give him the kind of latitude I might want in some other circumstance. More than that, I will ask that I come to possess the same commitment to justice and righteousness.

But let there be no doubt: Anger is dangerous. Indeed, eternally dangerous. The righteous anger that can compel someone to work and pray for a cause can become demonic anger that seeks to destroy the person representing the other side. The anger that takes someone to a public meeting where they stand to plead their case before a legislative body can turn sour, so that the speech leaves the issue and turns into vilification of those on the other side.

So what do I do with anger? If, as I have insisted, anger rightly used is essential to human progress and to social, economic, and political reform—but wrongly used is the combustible stuff that revolutionaries and tyrants exploit—how do I deal with it? That's where the psalmists are at their best, because the psalmists speak their minds with the recognition that they themselves stand under the judgment of God.

That realization is spoken most clearly and dramatically in the psalm that is before us just now. Psalm 139 is one of the most beautiful passages in the Bible; indeed, in all of literature. The psalmist spends most of the twenty-four verses—three-quarters of them—marveling at the omniscience of God. But it is not the omniscience of God in general, and surely not in philosophical or theological detachment. Far from it! David, the traditional author, is consumed by God's absolute knowledge of *David*. Mind you, it isn't an egotistical thing; this attention from God isn't important because of the status it gives him. The focus is all on God. The psalmist is altogether astonished that God would bother to know him so well and would be inclined to such exquisite detail.

O LORD, you have searched me and known me.
You know when I sit down and when I rise up;
      you discern my thoughts from far away. (Psalm 139:1-2)

Note that phrase "discern my thoughts," for here—as I
see it—is the heart of this psalm. The writer will find many
ways to describe the wonder of God's omniscience and
omnipresence, but the consuming issue is God's knowledge
of his thoughts. This knowledge is so great that "even before
a word is on my tongue, / O LORD, you know it completely"
(v. 4). The psalmist wasn't privy to our neurological studies
that measure the distance between a thought at some corner
of the brain and its expulsion at the tip of the tongue, but he
was intuitive enough to know that such a distance existed—
and more than that, that God stood monitor at that mystical
place.

He knew, too, that he could not flee from this presence.
Whether he went to heaven or to She'ol, whether with "the
wings of the morning" to the "farthest limits of the sea," or
to a place where he reasoned "the darkness shall cover me,"
no matter: "The darkness is as light to you" (vv. 8, 9, 11, 12).
How is it that God knows David (and you and me) so well?
Because "you knit me together in my mother's womb"; you
were there "when I was being made in secret, / intricately
woven in the depths of the earth" (vv. 13, 15). No wonder,
then, that he writes, "How weighty to me are your thoughts,
O God!" (v. 17).

Now, abruptly and disconcertingly, David changes themes.
He moves from his marveling at God's knowledge of David
and of David's thoughts to a violent prayer:

O that you would kill the wicked, O God,
      and that the bloodthirsty would depart from me—
those who speak of you maliciously,
      and lift themselves up against you for evil!

      (vv. 19-20)

At this point David gives full, eloquent vent to his anger:

Do I not hate those who hate you, O LORD?
    And do I not loathe those who rise up against you?
I hate them with perfect hatred;
    I count them my enemies. (vv. 21-22)

As readers, we see quickly that David feels he is on the side of God in his hating. He hates these people because they are God's enemies. Since they have risen up against God, "I count them my enemies." Perhaps he is not a full achiever in some of life's aspects, but in this he is an expert: "I hate them with a perfect hatred." This is a point at which he cannot be improved upon—this matter of his hatred for this unidentified enemy.

But any of us who observe human nature somewhat critically realize that it's very easy to baptize our prejudices and judgments. If we don't like something or someone or some cause, it's hard to imagine that God has poorer taste than we do, so God must surely hate this thing or person, too. And this psalmist, God bless him, was wise enough to see this dangerous potential in his thinking. So with wonderful wisdom, he shifts gears for the conclusion to his prayer:

Search me, O God, and know my heart;
    test me and know my thoughts.
See if there is any wicked way in me,
    and lead me in the way everlasting. (vv. 23-24)

If there's anything of the psalmist in you, you want to smile at this point. Having declared for eighteen verses how he marvels at God's knowledge of everything that is in his heart, he dares at last in the next four verses to tell God exactly how he feels about his enemies (whom he identifies, remember, as also being God's enemies). But having said, "I hate them with a perfect hatred," he hastens to add, "Have I said anything wrong? Have I spoken in any wickedness?"

This is the perfect prayer for the angry soul. It is the restraint that keeps the reformer from becoming the agent of violence. This prayer makes anger a tool for the achieving of God's will rather than the bludgeon of demonic destruction.

I repeat my earlier declaration. I doubt that any great victory for good, any human progress, has ever happened except as someone has become angry with the way things are. I applaud those persons who believed that slavery was a demonic villainy, and who threw their energy in the struggle to end it. Some years ago my neighbor, an economist, worked with the Lyndon Johnson administration in the "War on Poverty." As a scholar, he was uneasy with describing the economic reform program as a "war," and saw the language as primarily a public-relations gimmick. Perhaps so, but theologically the language was right; poverty is an evil, and those who oppose it go to battle to do so. Sadly, that war is far from won, even though we have many of the resources necessary for victory.

But! All of this energy of anger that we would invest to do good can so easily become an instrument of evil. Most great power is like this, ready to be exercised for either good or evil, and anger is one of nature's greatest energy forces. That's why the psalmist's prayer is utterly crucial. Without his understanding of the divine mind, the mind that knows us even before we have fully spoken our thoughts, and without his realization that our best human intentions and our highest commitment to abolishing evil are susceptible to human error, we are likely to do our most monstrous evil even as we enter battle committed to good. So while the psalmist prays for the victory of good and the destruction of evil, he never forgets his own capacity for evil. "Search me, O God, and know my heart; . . . See if there is any wicked way in me" (vv. 23-24).

But a question remains. What is the purpose of prayer in this struggle against evil? Why do the psalmists plead with God to destroy their enemies? Is there any place for such prayers?

The answer is profound, yet rather simple. We live in a world where there is a continual battle between good and evil. We see it in operation at every level of life: economics, politics, science, literature, international affairs, and human relations; but especially and most radically, within our own bodies, minds, and spirits. You and I are miniature battle-fields, microcosms of what is going on in the larger world around us.

So how do we fight this evil? By means almost as varied as the operations of evil. We fight evil by education, by political action, by economic reform, by petitions, and by marching in the streets.

And by *prayer*. There is something about evil that is beyond the reach of even the most enlightened education and the most advanced and earnest reform movements. Something of this evil resides in the human heart, with a tenacity so subtle that we are sometimes horrified by our own thoughts and our own complicity in ways of life that we despise. This is the realm of the spiritual. We do not fully understand it, and I dare to say that we never will; its most profound secrets are known only to God. But we know that it is real enough that we cannot possibly deal with it by only political, economic, and educational methods. We need the help of the spiritual. We need prayer.

No wonder, then, that when our Lord left us with a model prayer, it included, "Your kingdom come. / Your will be done, / on earth as it is in heaven" (Matthew 6:10). Our Lord gave us this prayer because it is as essential to our welfare as "Give us this day our daily bread," or "forgive us our debts" (Matthew 6:11-12). If we want God's kingdom to come, and if we want God's will to be done, it is not enough that we work for it, politicize for it, and educate for it; we must also *pray* for it, because there are elements in evil that cannot be dealt with in any other way.

This reminds us that there is nothing *tame* about prayer. It can be meditative, mind you, and comforting and quietly sustaining. But it engages in the battle of the ages. After all, prayer deals with matters of life, death, and eternity; it wrestles with hell. So of course it includes expressions of anger against all that violates the will and purposes of God.

I am grateful even unto eternity that my Dearest Friend cares enough about you and me and our universe that he engages with us in the battle against evil. I want a God who is angry with all that hurts and destroys, that cheapens and violates. I want to join with God in this battle. I need prayer to do so: prayer that is powerful enough to attack evil at its most subtle and hidden places, and prayer that is humble and perceptive enough to keep my anger in productive restraint.

Suggestions for Leading a Study of *Longing to Pray*

John D. Schroeder

This book by J. Ellsworth Kalas examines prayers from the book of Psalms to show how to better understand the nature of our eternal friendship with God. To assist you in facilitating a discussion group, this study guide was created to help make this experience beneficial for both you and members of your group. Here are some thoughts on how you can help your group:

1. Distribute the book to participants before your first meeting, and request that they come having read the first chapter. You may want to limit the size of your group to increase participation.

2. Begin your sessions on time. Your participants will appreciate your promptness. You may wish to begin your first session with introductions and a brief get-acquainted time. Start each session by reading aloud the snapshot summary of the chapter for the day.

3. Select discussion questions and activities in advance. Note that the first question is a general question designed to get discussion going. The last question is designed to summa-

rize the discussion. Feel free to change the order of the listed questions and to create your own questions. Allow a set amount of time for the questions and activities.

4. Remind your participants that all questions are valid as part of the learning process. Encourage their participation in discussion by saying there are no "wrong" answers and that all input will be appreciated. Invite them to share their thoughts, personal stories, and ideas as their comfort level allows.

5. Some questions may be more difficult to answer than others. If you ask a question and no one responds, begin the discussion by venturing an answer yourself. Then ask for comments and other answers. Remember that some questions may have multiple answers.

6. Ask the question "Why?" or "Why do you believe that?" to help continue a discussion and give it greater depth.

7. Give everyone a chance to talk. Keep the conversation moving. Occasionally you may want to direct a question to a specific person who has been quiet. "Do you have anything to add?" is a good follow-up question to ask another person. If the topic of conversation gets off track, move ahead by asking the next question in your study guide.

8. Before moving from questions to activities, ask group members if they have any questions that have not been answered. Remember that as a leader, you do not have to know all the answers. Some answers may come from group members. Other answers may even need a bit of research. Your job is to keep the discussion moving and to encourage participation.

9. Review the activity in advance. Feel free to modify it or to create your own activity. Encourage participants to try the "At home" activity.

10. Following the conclusion of the activity, close with a brief prayer, praying either the printed prayer from the study guide or a prayer of your own. If your group desires, pause for individual prayer petitions.

11. Be grateful and supportive. Thank group members for their ideas and participation.

12. You are not expected to be a "perfect" leader. Just do the best you can by focusing on the participants and the lesson. God will help you lead this group.

13. Enjoy your time together!

Suggestions for Participants

1. What you will receive from this study will be in direct proportion to your involvement. Be an active participant!

2. Please make it a point to attend all sessions and to arrive on time so that you can receive the greatest benefit.

3. Read the chapter and review the study guide questions prior to the meeting. You may want to jot down questions you have from the reading, and also answers to some of the study guide questions.

4. Be supportive and appreciative of your group leader as well as of the other members of your group. You are on a journey together.

5. Your participation is encouraged. Feel free to share your thoughts about the material being discussed.

6. Pray for your group and your leader.

CHAPTER 1
The Ultimate Friendship

Snapshot Summary

This chapter shows the value of having a strong friendship with God and how the prayers in the book of Psalms provide understanding of this friendship.

Reflection / Discussion Questions

1. In your own words, describe what friendship is, and what it means to be a friend.

2. Reflect on / discuss the following statement: "Friendship has more to do with desire than with design."

3. Briefly describe one friendship that has blessed your life.

4. What are some of the limitations of human friendship?

5. Why do we all need Divine Friendship?

6. Why is prayer an important ingredient in friendship with God?

7. What are some reasons that we might struggle with prayer?

8. What does J. Ellsworth Kalas say about the authorship and organization of the psalms?

9. What did the author say were some of the ways the book of Psalms can help us learn about prayer, God, and friendship?

10. What additional new insights about the psalms, prayer, or friendship did you receive from reading this chapter?

Activities

As a group: How human friendships differ from friendship with God. On a chalkboard or newsprint, write the words *Human* and *God,* and underneath them list the characteristics of that particular type of friendship. Discuss how the two types of friendship are similar and how they are different.

At home: Spend some time this week reading in the book of Psalms, in order to become more familiar with it.

Prayer: Dear God, thank you for the privilege of friendship with you. Help us nurture this friendship that we may grow through it. Show us how to be a true friend to you and to others. Open our eyes and ears so that we may learn the lessons found in the psalms. Amen.

CHAPTER 2

Secrets of Friendship: Candor

Snapshot Summary

This chapter shows the value of being sincere and open within a friendship. We need to be straightforward with our friends and honest with God in prayer.

Reflection / Discussion Questions

1. Explain what candor is, and give an example of it.
2. What is the difference between how you act and talk with an old friend and how you act and talk with a new friend or with someone you've just met?
3. Explain why friendship makes for candor.
4. Why is candor good? What does it add to a relationship?
5. According to the author, what makes Psalms the most candid book in the Bible?
6. Give some examples of how the psalms contain candor.
7. Name some persons with whom you feel you can be candid. What makes you feel this way about these particular persons?
8. Why can we, and why should we, be candid with God?
9. What are possible consequences of our not being candid?
10. Name one important point you learned about friendship, candor, or prayer from your reading or discussion of this chapter.

Activities

As a group: Search the psalms for more examples of candor. Talk about each example you find, and create a list of these examples including the chapter and verse where they can be found.

At home: Focus on being candid, open, and honest as you talk with God this week. Know that you can share anything with your Divine Friend.

Prayer: Dear God, thank you for showing us how candor sustains and enhances a friendship. Help us be completely honest with you and with others. Grant us courage to take risks in our relationships and to go beyond the superficial. May we be honest in prayer and a faithful friend to you. Amen.

CHAPTER 3
Secrets of Friendship: Time

Snapshot Summary

This chapter reminds us that friendships require an investment of time in order to deepen and grow, including the Divine Friendship we have with God.

Reflection / Discussion Questions

1. Why does friendship require time? Name a few of the reasons. What makes friendships worth the investment?

2. What does it mean to "take time to be holy"?

3. Reflect on / discuss how communing with God can be both "magnificently real" yet also intangible.

4. Do you agree with the author's statement that "we don't often know when we have completed God's purpose in our prayers? Explain your answer.

5. According to the author, what is interesting and noteworthy about the structure and form of the psalms?

6. How do the psalms teach us about the importance of time?

7. In what ways is repetition good for a friendship? In what ways can repetition be detrimental in prayer?

8. What often causes us to be in a hurry when we pray? What do we miss when we hurry?

9. Why is it wise to schedule prayer into your day?

10. What does it mean to you to pray in a way that involves both heart and mind?

Activities

As a group: Use newsprint and crayons or markers to create a poster that reflects investing time in our friendship with God. Each member of the group may contribute his or her own ideas or design.

At home: Be intentional about scheduling time for prayer on each day of the coming week.

Prayer: Dear God, thank you for giving us the gift of time. Help us use time to build friendships that are strong and mutually fulfilling. Grant us love, patience, and understanding as we seek to grow in our relationships. Slow us down, and help us pray more and worry less. In Jesus' name. Amen.

CHAPTER 4
Secrets of Friendship: Beauty

Snapshot Summary

This chapter is about opening our eyes to beauty and expressing beauty within friendships, both human and divine.

Reflection / Discussion Questions

1. Define *beauty,* and give some examples of it. Is the saying true that "beauty is in the eye of the beholder"? Explain.

2. List some ways in which beauty is celebrated.

3. In what ways do you believe you personally express beauty, or in what ways would you like to be able to do so?

4. Reflect on / discuss how beauty can be expressed within a friendship.

5. What, in your opinion, are some of the characteristics of beautiful language?

6. How do the psalms bring beauty to the Divine Friendship?

7. In what ways do you find beauty expressed in Psalm 119?

8. What observations does the author make about public prayer?

9. Should our prayers be beautiful? Explain your answer.

10. As the author suggests, what is it about beauty that God finds most pleasing?

Activities

As a group: Examine Psalm 119 to locate words and phrases of beauty.

At home: Do something beautiful for God this week.

Prayer: Dear God, you are the source of beauty and of all things beautiful. Help us see and enjoy the beauty all around us. Remind us that all people are beautiful and that each person is a child of God. Show us how to bring beauty into our relationships and how to love one another just as you love us. Amen.

CHAPTER 5
Secrets of Friendship:
Place, Posture, and Punctuality

Snapshot Summary

This chapter looks at the formalities of prayer and how they enhance friendship.

Reflection / Discussion Questions

1. Give examples of some instinctive "rules" we observe in our friendships, and explain why these are significant or important.
2. Define *posture* as it relates to prayer, and explain why it matters.
3. How do you determine which posture is right for prayer?
4. What can we learn from the psalms about the *place* in which we pray?
5. Why is it good to have a set place for daily communion with God?
6. Where do you most like to pray, and why?
7. Does it matter *when* we pray? What answers do the psalmists provide?
8. What time of day or night do you like to pray, and why?
9. Reflect on / discuss the following statement: "Time, place, and posture are not determinative in power, but they can enhance our effectiveness in prayer."
10. How has prayer strengthened your friendship with God?

Activities

As a group: Let each participant create his or her own personal "psalm" that reflects elements of place, posture, and time as they relate to prayer. Share your psalm with the rest of the group.

At home: Experiment with different places, postures, and times of the day or night in your prayer time this week.

Prayer: Dear God, thank you for the opportunity to learn more about formalities of prayer and how they relate to our friendship with you. Help us take prayer more seriously and be more intentional about it. Show us how to nurture friendship and to learn from the psalmists what it truly means to have a strong friendship with you. Amen.

CHAPTER 6
Secrets of Friendship: Exuberance

Snapshot Summary

This chapter looks at the expression of excitement and joyous abundance as aspects of friendship, and how we communicate them through prayer.

Reflection / Discussion Questions

1. Share a time when you experienced exuberance.
2. List some common exuberant words or actions.
3. Is exuberance contagious? Explain your answer.
4. Why is exuberance so common in the psalms?
5. What is the secret of exuberance, according to the author; in other words, what does it require of us? Explain your answer.
6. Reflect on / discuss the connection between faith and exuberance.
7. Why are some people afraid to enter the exuberance of a friendship?
8. What is the mood of the psalmist in Psalm 96, and what are the reasons for his mood?
9. Explain how exuberance can be a way of life.
10. List some ways you can express exuberance in your friendship with God.

Activities

As a group: Use a hymnal or other worship songbook to locate songs of praise that contain exuberance. Select and share favorite phrases from these hymns.

At home: Practice exuberance in your relationship with God and with others this week.

Prayer: Dear God, thank you for times of celebration during which we feel especially connected to you or to the friends you have given us. Help us enjoy life and all that you have provided. Show us how to communicate our joy in prayer to you and in our words and actions between one another. May we treasure our friends and our relationship with you. Amen.

CHAPTER 7
Secrets of Friendship: Specificity

Snapshot Summary

This chapter shows that our praying and our friendship with God are significantly deepened when we move beyond generalities to name specific persons, specific needs, specific sins, and specific wonders.

Reflection / Discussion Questions

1. Do you believe we live in a superficial society today? Explain your answer.
2. Why do we often use "general" terms? What makes specifics better?
3. Reflect on / discuss how friendships might die from laziness.
4. Reflect on / discuss ways in which specificity can enhance a friendship.
5. According to the author, why would "The Lord is *my* shepherd" be considered a more effective form of prayer than "The Lord is *our* shepherd"?
6. Give some examples of praying in generalities.
7. Why were the psalmists not content with generalities?
8. Share a time when you were specific with God in prayer.

9. How and why does it help our relationship with God to be specific?

10. What does the author say are some of the benefits of mentioning specific names to God when praying for others?

Activities

As a group: Use Bibles to locate specific promises God offers to believers. Share several examples.

At home: Think about the way in which you talk to God. Strive to be specific with God this week in your prayers.

Prayer: Dear God, thank you for your attention to detail. You know everything about us, every last detail. Help us strive to learn more about you and your will for us. Show us how to speak to you with confidence and directness. Remind us that we can talk to you about anything because of your love for us. Amen.

CHAPTER 8
Secrets of Friendship: Wonder and Witness

Snapshot Summary

This chapter explores the connection between the awe we have for God and how we express it to others.

Reflection / Discussion Questions

1. In your own words, explain the meaning of *wonder*, and give an example of it.

2. Reflect on / discuss how wonder applies to human friendship.

3. Share a time when you viewed someone with wonder.

4. In what ways can you be a witness on behalf of your friends—someone who believes in them and supports them?

5. Why do you think the psalmists had such a strong sense of wonder?

6. How do you feel after reading some of the psalms within this chapter?

7. Reread Psalm 23. Why do you think this psalm is such a powerful psalm of witness for so many?

8. Do you tend to think of God as immanent and approachable, or as transcendent and eternal? Are there tensions for you between those two views? Explain.

9. Other than writing a psalm, what are some ways in which we can witness to others about God's wonder?

10. What new insight did you gain from this chapter about how to talk to God?

Activities

As a group: Create a psalm of praise to God, with each person contributing one line.

At home: Locate and reflect on examples in the Bible that speak of God's wonder. This week, focus on letting your words and actions with others serve as a witness to God's wonder, and a witness to your friendship with God.

Prayer: Dear God, you are an awesome God! Help us rely upon you and lift up your name, even when—*especially* when—life's circumstances are hard to bear. Thank you for your goodness, your power, and your glory. Grant us your love and peace, we pray. Amen.

CHAPTER 9

Secrets of Friendship: Gratitude

Snapshot Summary

This chapter shows why gratitude is essential in the language of holy friendship we call prayer.

Reflection / Discussion Questions

1. Reflect on / discuss the following statement: "Gratitude is the recognition that no one is a solitary achiever, that no one has accumulated success or wealth unaided."
2. List some of the reasons for feeling gratitude toward God.
3. How does gratitude make life better?
4. Share a time when you felt and expressed gratitude.
5. Reflect on / discuss why gratitude is an essential component of prayer.
6. Name some examples of how gratitude can wrongly be used as a means to an end.
7. Reread Psalm 92 and explain how this psalm reflects gratitude to God. Give some examples.
8. Reread Psalm 118. What can we learn about gratitude from this psalm?
9. Name some reasons why we sometimes lack gratitude.
10. List some ways we can express gratitude to God and to others.

Activities

As a group: Create your own five-sentence "psalms" that expresses gratitude. Share the psalms among the group.

At home: Create a "gratitude list" of blessings received by God.

Prayer: Dear God, thank you for your many blessings, more than we can count. Thank you for friendships, laughter, the beauty of nature, animals, family, fresh air, and the food and shelter we enjoy each day. We are truly blessed. Help us share these blessings with others and grow closer to you. Amen.

CHAPTER 10
Secrets of Friendship: Repentance

Snapshot Summary

This chapter looks at human imperfection and the need we have to say "I'm sorry" to God and to our fellow human beings.

Reflection / Discussion Questions

1. List some reasons why people seek repentance.
2. How is saying "I'm sorry" also a declaration of trust?
3. Why is "I'm sorry" so difficult to say?
4. As you are comfortable doing so, share a time when you said you were sorry to God or to a friend.
5. Why is repentance a necessary ingredient of friendship?
6. If you are on the receiving end of an apology, what is your obligation?
7. Reflect on / discuss the meaning of the following statement: "Repentance is key to the knowing of ourselves."
8. In what ways does soul searching provide comfort to you? In what ways is it challenging?
9. Name some things we can learn about repentance from the psalmists.
10. Reflect on / discuss why the need to repent is often greater than the need to be forgiven.

Activities

As a group: Search the psalms to create a list of words and phrases that reflect repentance.

At home: In your prayers this week, focus on repentance. Remember that you can be completely open and honest with God.

Prayer: Dear God, thank you for forgiving our many mistakes and sins. Help us refrain from what we know is wrong and, instead, do what is right. May we turn away from sin and turn to you in prayer for all our needs. Also help us be forgiving of others and seek the healing that comes from saying "I'm sorry" when we've caused someone to hurt. Amen.

CHAPTER 11
Secrets of Friendship: Helplessness

Snapshot Summary

This chapter examines the situations and feelings associated with helplessness that accompany our friendship with God.

Reflection / Discussion Questions

1. How does it feel to be helpless?
2. How does our culture view helplessness?
3. Share a time when you experienced helplessness.
4. Explain why helplessness is a key element in our eternal friendship with God.
5. In what ways has God chosen to take on the element of helplessness?
6. How does Psalm 18 demonstrate and celebrate helplessness?
7. Reflect on / discuss the following statement: "We probably know very little about ourselves until we see what we are like when backed into a corner."
8. How does helplessness before God make us less vulnerable to the judgments of others?
9. Explain how David found greatness through helplessness.
10. What additional insights about helplessness did you gain from your reading or discussion of this chapter?

Activities

As a group: Create a list of constructive actions you can take when you feel helpless.

At home: Offer your help to someone who needs it this week, and reflect on ways to share your strength through being a humble servant.

Prayer: Dear God, thank you for always being ready to help us at any time, day or night, in any situation. We can always come to you in prayer. Help us be there for others, just as you are there for us in times of trouble. Show us how to be your good and faithful servants. Amen.

CHAPTER 12
Secrets of Friendship: Anger

Snapshot Summary

This chapter examines aspects of anger and anger's role in our friendship with God and others.

Reflection / Discussion Questions

1. Reflect on / discuss why anger is an important element of friendship.
2. Name some things that make you angry.
3. Share a time when you got angry over how someone was treated.
4. How can reading the psalms help us when we are angry or hurt?
5. Explain why anger is essential to human progress.
6. How can you deal with anger constructively?
7. What are some lessons we can learn about anger from reading Psalm 139?

8. What is the purpose of prayer in the struggle against evil?

9. If a friend is angry with you, what should you do?

10. What insights did you gain into prayer and your relationship with God from your reading or discussion of this book?

Activities

As a group: Have a graduation time for members of your small group. Create personalized completion certificates, then exchange them and write messages of friendship and encouragement.

At home: Write a letter to God this week. Put your feelings down on paper in the form of a prayer. Reflect on what you have written.

Prayer: Dear God, thank you for your loving friendship and for being with us at all times. Thank you for giving us the opportunity to talk with you in prayer. Help us remember that we may express ourselves fully and share all things with you, just as the psalmists did. Teach us to listen for your voice as you speak to us and to open ourselves to your guidance. Help us be a faithful friend to you and to others. In Jesus' name. Amen.